Bounding from joyous confidence to occasional appre-
hension, from dreams and hopes to feelings of inadequacy,
the moods of a mother-to-be are volatile and varied. Each of
these moods is masterfully captured in these Bible-based
devotions and guided into paths of assurance and
commitment.

Many guides offer technical and scientific counsel to the
expectant mother, but few are concerned with her spiritual
well-being. Full of gratitude and rejoicing, these daily devotions will enable a woman to truly be joyfully expectant.

# Joyfully

# Expectant

## MEDITATIONS BEFORE BABY COMES

## Helen Kooiman Hosier

Fleming H. Revell Company
Old Tappan, New Jersey

The poems "In Christ Neither Greek Nor Jew" (p. 48) and "A Mother's Gift" (pp. 98–9) are reprinted by permission of the author, Naomi Carr Lance.

The poem "Suppose," by Martha Snell Nicholson, which appears on pp. 83–4, is used by permission of Moody Press, Moody Bible Institute of Chicago.

Scripture quotations in this publication, unless otherwise identified, are from *The King James Version of the Bible*.

Scripture passages identified as RSV are from *The Revised Standard Version of the Bible*, copyrighted 1946 and 1952 by the Division of Christian Education, National Council of Churches, and used by permission.

Scripture passages identified as PHILLIPS are from *The New Testament in Modern English*, by J.B. Phillips, copyrighted 1958. Used by permission of The Macmillan Company, New York, and Geoffrey Bles Ltd., London.

Scripture passages identified as BERKELEY are from *The Holy Bible— The Berkeley Version in Modern English*, copyrighted 1958 and 1959 by Zondervan Publishing House, Grand Rapids, Mich., and used by permission.

Scripture passages identified as LIVING LETTERS are from *Living Letters*, by Kenneth N. Taylor, copyrighted 1962 by Tyndale House Publishers, Wheaton, Ill., and used by permission.

Scripture passages identified as AMPLIFIED are from *The Amplified Old Testament*, copyrighted 1958 by Zondervan Publishing House, Grand Rapids, Mich., and used by permission.

ISBN 0-8007-5060-8

*To*
*my own precious*
*"heritage of the Lord,"*
*to their grandmothers,*
*and to*
*all mothers*

# Introduction

Nine months, to the expectant mother, can be some of the longest and most uncomfortable months of her life. However, these months can be a time of spiritual growth, of close communion with and dependence on God, and, most of all, a time of joyous expectancy.

Mrs. Hosier has beautifully dealt with the concerns, joys, and hopes of the mother-to-be, and at the same time skillfully guides the reader in a meaningful and appropriate Bible study, beginning with Genesis and going through the Bible. What a perfect combination of progression!

Those of us who already have children — there are five in my household—will find ourselves wishing that such a book had been available when we were expecting. We will also find that there is much to challenge us to renewed dedication in our God-given task of rearing and guiding our children, with His help, into paths of right and truth.

If you have a bedside table, I'd suggest that you keep this practical little volume on it. Start each day with the Lord, and you'll find your "waiting days" to be the most wonderful days of your life.

*Mrs. Cliff (Billie) Barrows*

# Acknowledgments

A special word of thanks is due Dr. Martin H. Sterk for reading and verifying the accuracy of pages 73 and 74. Profoundest gratitude is owed to Lenore Gustafson for reading the original manuscript, and for her prayers and encouragement; and to all my dear friends who also encouraged and prayed.

# Preface

Little Debby came rushing into the house. "Mommy! **Oh, Mommy!** The neighbors down the street, the ones who have so many children, have a new baby!" Mommy was surprised. "Just think, Mommy," Debby said, "they still have their other babies, and now they have the new baby!"

That was part of Mommy's reason for being surprised. It was true, the youngest in that family was not much more than a year old. "Oh dear," Mommy said, "whatever will that woman do with another baby in the house?"

Mommy was thinking aloud of the endless mounds of diapers and all the other work involved with a baby. Not that Mommy didn't love babies—goodness knows she did! But Mommy was lovingly concerned.

Little Debby looked at her Mommy seriously, trying to understand. Then she cocked her head to one side, momentarily puzzled, but quickly brightened and said, "Oh, I know, next time they have to give a wedding gift, or a birthday present, they can give one of the babies. We'd take a baby for a present, huh, Mommy?"

Mommy was startled; in fact, she was speechless! Debby continued, noticing her Mommy's expression: "Well, Mommy, after all, you said a baby was God's best gift!"

So He was: Jesus was God's best Gift. And every little baby you and I have, or may have, is but another reminder that the most precious Gift heaven ever gave to earth came in the form of a Baby. This was Love personified.

Now you are to have a baby. Or, perhaps, you are going to have another baby. Whether this is your first baby, or your umpteenth, to you has been given a great privilege, that of bearing children. For every little baby who is born is but another reminder that these little people, so fresh from God, are tokens of His love.

In no way does this book pretend to be an exhaustive study of "expectant motherhood." It is simply a collection of my own personal thoughts relating to the expectant mother; they are drawn from Bible narratives, verses, and meaningful passages.

I have felt the need for such a book four different times. It is with this in mind that I have prayerfully written these meditations. Many of them have been written while our youngest little heritage of the Lord was lying in his crib near at hand; some while he was sitting nearby, often right under the typewriter table; and some of the final ones while he, in typical all-boy fashion, was running about the yard.

May your heart be blessed in these wonderful days of waiting that lie ahead. May you be encouraged, too. May God's Presence and His love be very real.

*Helen Kooiman Hosier*

## Whispers of Maternity

O, hush, little wild bird, trill softly your song—
The shadows are falling . . . the day has been long:
All purple and crimson and gold, glow the skies—
And under my heart . . . another heart lies!

O, hush, sportive west wind, blow soft o'er the lea,
All laden with perfume and summer for me:
Blow lightly and faintly as from Southern skies—
For under my heart . . . a little heart lies!

O, smile on us, Heaven, bend low to us now—
The seal of your glory, place here on my brow:
For twilight is falling . . . the tender day dies—
And under my heart . . . a dearer heart lies!

MARCIA RAY

*Lo, children are an heritage of the Lord: and the fruit of the womb is his reward. As arrows are in the hand of a mighty man; so are children of the youth. Happy is the man that hath his quiver full of them* ... PSALM 127:3–5

There is only one other gift from the Lord that is greater than the heritage of children; that is the gift of salvation God has freely given to us in His only Son. How great and how good are His gifts!

Today, praise and thank God for this heritage, that you can bear children. Today, thank Him for His gift of eternal life through Jesus Christ, and for all His gifts.

*And she shall bring forth a son, and thou shalt call his name Jesus: for he shall save his people from their sins.*

MATTHEW 1:21

God's best Gift came into this world in the very same way your baby will come to you: Mary brought forth a son; you will bring forth a child. God's ways are perfect. Childbearing and childbirth are parts of His perfect ways. Just as God entrusted His Son to a chosen woman, so He has entrusted the life of this unborn child to you.

Pray today that God will give you good health and the virtues that the mother of Christ showed as she awaited the birth of her Firstborn.

*. . . she was the mother of all living.* GENESIS 3:20

Eden was the cradle of the human race. That is where Adam's wife Eve became the first mother.

15

Motherhood is a holy calling. There is a saying, "God couldn't be everywhere, so He made mothers." We become mothers through the miracle of childbirth. And this is a part of God's will for us.

Not all mothers are good mothers. The miracle of a biological process, whereby a child is placed in our care and keeping, does not necessarily make us good. Eve, the mother of all living, was no exception. We can, however, be the kind of mothers God intends for us to be as we ask for and accept His Way and His will. This calls for obedience and trust.

At my mother's knee I learned the song "Trust and Obey"; ever since, it has been my favorite. Today, sing or read it aloud. Mean what you say, and let this be a special moment of rededication to His will for your life, and the life of your unborn child, as you yield in trust and promise to obey.

*And Adam knew Eve his wife; and she conceived, and bare Cain, and said, I have gotten a man from the Lord.* GENESIS 4:1

Eve acknowledged the fact that her firstborn was from the Lord. The fact that you, too, will be a mother calls for the same response. This is a wonderful opportunity for you to give witness to your faith in God and your love for Christ.

If you have not already done so, you will soon be sharing the good news that you are "expecting" a little newcomer. What better way for you to make the happy announcement than to say, "We are going to receive a baby from the Lord!"

Pray that your announcement will warm the hearts of others. Pray, too, that others will realize that you are acknowledging God as the Giver and Sustainer of life.

*. . . then began men to call upon the name of the Lord.*
GENESIS 4:26

A baby makes a difference—in many ways! Did the birth of one of Adam's and Eve's grandchildren make a difference in the lives of its parents, Seth and his wife? Did it make a difference in the other lives? The Bible tells that after the birth of Seth's son Enos, men began to call upon the name of the Lord.

Is there anything quite as heart-warming and heart-touching as the utter helplessness of an infant? What joy a baby brings! The days preceding the arrival of your baby can be days of prospective joy for you, your husband, and other members of your families. Pray that these days will make a difference in the lives of others as they see your joy.

Do you have family members, friends, or neighbors who are not now calling upon the Lord? What God accomplished before, He can do again!

*And he called his name Noah, saying, This same shall comfort us concerning our work and toil of our hands, because of the ground which the Lord hath cursed.* GENESIS 5:29

In Biblical times great stress was laid upon the meaning of a name. Noah is a case in point. Certainly if anyone lived up to his name, it was Noah. (Read Genesis 8:15-22; think upon the meaning of verse 21.)

If you are like most prospective parents, you will be doing a good bit of name-searching in the coming months. The writer of Proverbs (22:1) tells us that "A good name is rather to be chosen than great riches. . . ." Whatever name you choose to call your child, it is not too early for you to pray that he will choose to be called a child of God!

Jesus said, ". . . rejoice, because your names are written in heaven" (Luke 10:20). Today—rejoice!

*And God blessed Noah and his sons, and said unto them, Be fruitful, and multiply, and replenish the earth.* GENESIS 9:1

God's blessings never cease! The very fact that you are going to have a child is but a single evidence of God's blessing. Your fruitfulness was included in God's promise to bless Noah and his progeny, who, He said, would multiply and replenish the earth. Turn to the roll-call-of-faith chapter, Hebrews 11; read of those faithful, fruitful ones, the fathers of old.

Thank God that He keeps His promises, and that His blessings never cease.

*And I will make of thee a great nation, and I will bless thee, and make thy name great; . . . and in thee shall all the families of the earth be blessed.* GENESIS 12:2–3

God called Abram, blessed him, and gave him the name "Abraham." The family God is going to give to you belongs to "all the families of the earth," about whom God spoke to faithful Abraham.

Thank God for His provision for "families."

*Is any thing too hard for the Lord?* GENESIS 18:14

Sarah laughed at the prospect that she would bear a child. But Sarah learned that there is nothing too hard for the Lord!

The fears Sarah must have felt at the thought of having a child in her old age were normal. The fears many women have while carrying children are not so different from those Sarah experienced. Can we learn, however, from Sarah?

Yes, I think we can learn from this woman who said, "Is any thing too hard for the Lord?" Trust God with all of your heart; turn your fears over to Him. He will undertake for you, even as He did for Abraham's wife.

Today read Genesis 21.

*. . . they blessed Rebekah, and said unto her, Thou art our sister, be thou the mother of thousands of millions, and let thy seed possess the gate of those which hate them.* GENESIS 24:60

Rebekah never knew her mother-in-law, Sarah. But how she must have thanked God over and over again for giving to Sarah a son, the man who was Rebekah's husband, Isaac. Hers is a beautiful story; it is a story of the first narrated marriage ceremony (v. 58) in the Bible. If Sarah had lived, I am sure

18

the relationship between these two women would have been very good.

The seed of Rebekah and Isaac and their generations are numberless. The births of Esau and Jacob, the twins, begins the story of the struggle of two nations (Genesis 25:21–28).

Today, if possible, visit, call, or write your mother-in-law. Tell her how thankful you are for her son, your husband. Share with her your joy, your hopes for your unborn child —her grandchild.

*And Leah conceived, and bare a son, . . . and she said, Now will I praise the Lord . . .* GENESIS 29:32–35

Leah became Jacob's wife through her father Laban's deceitfulness. Nothwithstanding this deceit, the Lord allowed Leah to bear Jacob six sons and a daughter. But she had to share her husband. The very thought of sharing one's husband with other women is totally repulsive to our Christian society today. Yet, it was not an uncommon thing in early Biblical times, and it was accepted.

Jacob loved Rachel, Leah's sister. This is a love story without equal, for here was a man who was willing to work and wait fourteen years for the woman he dearly loved. (Read Genesis 29.) Rachel, too, became Jacob's wife.

Leah's lot was certainly not the happiest, in spite of the fact that she bore children and Rachel did not. But there came a time, after the birth of her fourth son, when Leah could say, "Now will I praise the Lord. . . ." In the Book of Psalms we are reminded that ". . . praise is comely for the upright" (33:1). Perhaps Leah would have been happier if she had praised the Lord sooner!

Praise the Lord that you have conceived. How long has it been since you really offered unto Him loving praise for *all* that He has done? Today try this experiment: just praise God; pray only in praise—no petitions, no asking for bless-

19

ings for self or others. You will be amazed. "It is a good thing to give thanks unto the Lord, and to sing praises unto thy name . . . (Psalm 92:1).

*And God remembered Rachel, and God hearkened to her, and opened her womb. And she conceived, and bare a son; and said, God hath taken away my reproach.* GENESIS 30:22–23

Rachel, with deepest longings, must have prayerfully pleaded to the Lord for children. "God hearkened to her," and her son Joseph in due time was born.

God has hearkened to you, also. Your prayers have not gone unanswered. This would be a good time to study the many references to prayer in your Bible. Here are just a few: Acts 6:4; Hebrew 4:16; Philippians 4:6; James 5:16; John 14:13–14.

*. . . thy name shall not be called any more Jacob, but Israel shall be thy name, . . . a company of nations shall be of thee, and kings shall come out of thy loins.* GENESIS 35:10–11

Kings came forth from the loins of Jacob. A president may come from yours—or a missionary; a doctor, perhaps; a scientist; an artist; a poet; a nurse; or a writer. Jesus was a Carpenter.

It matters not what the ultimate vocations of our children will be, as long as you and I have taught them: " . . . whatsoever ye do, do it heartily, as to the Lord, and not unto men" (Colossians 3:23).

*She hath been more righteous than I . . .* GENESIS 38:26

Do you know who was the first woman mentioned in the genealogy of our Lord? Her name was Tamar. Tamar sold the dearest, most precious thing a woman has—her honor, virtue, and purity—for "a kid of the goats." To understand what this woman did, one must review the old Jewish customs.

20

Tamar was married to a son of Judah. Judah, the Word tells us, was a son of Jacob. Then Tamar's husband died, and according to the custom Tamar could not marry anyone outside the family as long as there was someone within the family who could marry her and raise up seed to their brother.

In process of time, Judah's wife died. Meanwhile Tamar was getting weary of waiting for Judah's youngest son Shelah to marry her. She therefore outwitted her father-in-law by posing as a girl of the streets. (Read the entire story in Genesis 38.)

Why does the Bible record such episodes? It does so to speak of sin and uncleanness in such a way as to make us hate them. It is an amazing thought that He who knew no sin, and in whom there was no sin, came to seek and save sinners—and His genealogy can be traced back to Judah and Tamar.

Judah and Tamar stand as monuments of God's pardoning mercy. This mercy is freely proffered to all who will believe and accept.

*And the woman took the child, and nursed it*   EXODUS 2:9

Can you imagine the fear that must have gripped the heart of Jochebed, the mother of Moses, in the months preceding the birth of her baby? It was a time of great stress for the Hebrew people living in bondage in Egypt. The wicked pharaoh had passed an edict ordering every son born to Hebrew women to be cast into the river. If ever girl babies were wanted, it must have been then!

Pharaoh's edict was designed to exterminate the Jewish people. But God had other plans! Every family was waiting, hoping for someone to deliver them from the cruel bondage. Jochebed's infant was to become the man of the hour. But it was the foundation of character and fear of God which Jochebed instilled into the heart of Moses during his tender years (while she acted as nursemaid for Pharaoh's daughter) that made the difference.

Determine now that even as Moses' mother had to cast her

three-month-old child adrift, you, too, will cast your child into the care of God.

*If men strive, and hurt a woman with child, so that her fruit depart from her, and yet no mischief follow: he shall be surely punished, according as the woman's husband will lay upon him; and he shall pay as the judges determine.* EXODUS 21:22

Application of the principles of the Ten Commandments are given in this and succeeding chapters in the Book of Exodus. Careful reading shows the beginning of a great moral movement.

Human life is a sacred thing. A woman with child, then as now, was to be treated with thoughtfulness and care.

Share this thought with your husband. Together, thank God for these details in His Word that emphasize the sanctity of human life.

*. . . offer it before the Lord, and make an atonement for her . . .* LEVITICUS 12:7

G. Campbell Morgan, that great Bible expositor, in explaining this chapter dealing with the beginning of life, states that the religious aspects of childbirth are unquestionably of permanent value.

He goes on to explain that in former times it was required that women be separated from the rest of the people for a specific period following childbirth. Dr. Morgan suggests that this was a recognition of the fact that the whole human race is sinful, and a consequence of this is the fact that every child is born in sin.

In those days a new mother could not take part in the privileges of worship until burnt offering presentations had been made. God, however, did provide a way of restoration to communion with Him for the mother. How gracious God is!

No longer do mothers have to undergo such offerings for their purifying. Jesus Christ made the final offering of His own life, and you are covered by His blood sacrifice if you have accepted Him as your Saviour.

Aren't you thankful? Tell Him so!

*The Law possessed only a dim outline of the benefits Christ would bring, and did not actually reproduce them. Consequently it was incapable of perfecting the souls of those who offered their regular annual sacrifices. . . . the blood of bulls and goats cannot really remove the guilt of sin. . . . Therefore, when Christ entered the world, he says:*

*Sacrifice and offering Thou wouldest not;*
*But a body didst Thou prepare for Me;*
*In whole burnt offerings and sacrifices for sin thou*
     *hadst no pleasure:*
*Then said I, Lo, I am come*
*(In the roll of the book it is written of Me)*
*To do Thy will, O God.* HEBREWS 10:1, 4, 5–7, PHILLIPS

Here is the Christmas story in miniature, as it were. Again we see what God's greatest Gift to mankind has done for us. And He came as a Baby.

In the Old Testament days, animals were required as sacrificial sin-offerings. But now that the Baby had come, the sacrifice of animals was on its way out. The Easter story comes into focus here, also, for we are told: ". . . we are sanctified through the offering of the body of Jesus Christ once for all" (Hebrews 10:10).

Sanctification means simply that we have been made holy by the offering of the Body of Christ. Meditate on this.

*And when the people complained, it displeased the Lord . . .*
NUMBERS 11:1

God does not cherish His people's complaints! To complain against God is sin. God dealt with sins of this nature among

23

the wandering Israelites, and He will deal with our sins of this sort, also.

There are times when a woman expecting a child wants very much to complain. She may even feel justified in her complaints; surely the discomforts of childbearing can be very real. But perhaps we can learn from the Old Testament record, and put forth greater effort to control our complaints.

We are told, "Cast thy burden upon the Lord, and he shall sustain thee . . ." (Psalm 55:22). We are reminded to be "Casting all your care upon him, for he careth for you" (I Peter 5:7). Do it today!

*For the life of the flesh is in the blood: and I have given it to you upon the altar to make an atonement for your souls: for it is the blood that maketh an atonement for the soul.*
LEVITICUS 17:11

After I returned home with our new baby daughter, our third child, I experienced something that made this verse very meaningful.

I had to be rushed back to the hospital because I was severely hemorrhaging; even while I was in a semi-conscious, very weakened condition, this verse came clearly into my thoughts. I knew I would die soon if fresh blood were not received and appropriated by my body. But I also knew—and the realization then was sweet—that Someone had shed His blood for me long ago, so that when I came to the moment of death, my soul had been atoned for by Him.

God spared my life; but He did not spare the life of His Son: "He that spared not his own Son, but delivered him up for us all, how shall he not with him also freely give us all things?" (Romans 8:32).

Today pray for your doctor. Continue to pray for him and for those who will attend you at the time of your delivery. Thank God, too, for the knowledge and skill with which medical science has been blessed. Then read the entire chapter of Romans 8, and thank God for the blood that atones.

*So it was alway: the cloud covered it by day, and the appearance of fire by night.* NUMBERS 9:16

Have you ever tried to imagine what it would have been like to have been a woman in the days of the wilderness wanderings? Can you imagine expecting a baby under such circumstances? I am certain we would agree that conditions for the expectant mother were not made easier by the wilderness walk. I am sure, too, that we would have welcomed the sight of the cloud leading by day, and the fire by night. Such guidance by the Lord Himself would have comforted and reassured us, even as it did the wandering Israelites.

The movement of the camp of Israel was guided by sight then, and by ear when the trumpet was sounded as the signal to move on. Today Christians are guided by faith. The Bible tells us: "For we walk by faith, not by sight" (II Corinthians 5:7). Today Christ does not call us with the mighty blast of a trumpet, but He speaks gently to us through His Word, through His ministers, through the printed page. He is calling still, through His Holy Spirit, in these and various ways. He wants to speak to you now, in this blessed experience of coming parenthood.

Read Hebrews 3; take special note of verse 15.

*Rise up, Lord, and let thine enemies be scattered; and let them that hate thee flee before thee.* NUMBERS 10:35

Here is a verse that is still recited today in Jewish synagogues. It was a recognition then, as now, that Moses and the people knew everything was in God's hands. And the Israelites dread of their enemies was real.

Christian concern today regarding the menace of communism and other forces of evil is equally real. Those approaching parenthood—whether this be their first child, second or third—find themselves wondering just what kind of a world they are bringing this child into.

How good it is to know that God is still on the throne, that the Most High ruleth, and that His perfect will in this world is going to be accomplished! Our own eternal safety and well-being, and that of our children, are in His hands. Let this prayer, spoken long ago by Moses, become our prayer, also.

*Know therefore this day, and consider it in thine heart, that the Lord he is God in heaven above, and upon the earth beneath: there is none else. Thou shalt keep therefore his statutes, and his commandments, which I command thee this day, that it may go well with thee, and with thy children after thee, and that thou mayest prolong thy days upon the earth, which the Lord thy God giveth thee, for ever.*

DEUTERONOMY 4:39–40

The Bible tells us elsewhere that God is not slack concerning His promises. When we are told that it will be well with our children, we can accept this in faith, believing. We accept it on the basis of what Christ did for us (Galatians 3).

We are God's children because of our faith in Christ. If we are faithful in training these children whom God entrusts to us in the ways of truth as revealed in His Word, then we can rest confidently in His promises.

For a better understanding of these rich truths, read the six chapters in the Book of Galatians.

*. . . he will also bless the fruit of thy womb . . .*

DEUTERONOMY 7:13

God is greater than our circumstances and seemingly insurmountable obstacles. Did He not prove this to the wandering Jews? How often has He shown this to you?

When the first signs of life are felt 'neath our heart, how joyful we are! God has blessed the fruit of our womb! As those signs of life become stronger, and the stirrings more

26

frequent, we know even more surely that God is blessing us.

In your preparations for the arrival of your baby, do not exclude Him who has blessed you. Ask God to make each one in your family ready to receive the blessing He gives.

*And the Lord thy God will circumcise thine heart, and the heart of thy seed, to love the Lord thy God with all thine heart, and with all thy soul, that thou mayest live.*

DEUTERONOMY 30:6

Physical circumcision couldn't get the world out of Israel then any more than it can today. This Scripture speaks of regeneration, which means to be reborn spiritually.

Paul's explanation to the people of his time made very clear what spiritual circumcision was: ". . . circumcision is that of the heart, in the spirit, and not in the letter . . ." (Romans 2:29).

A modern translation reads: "God is not looking for those who cut their bodies in actual body circumcision, but He is looking for those with changed hearts and minds" (LIVING LETTERS).

The Word tells us that God will accomplish this change in our hearts, *and in* the hearts of our seed. Do you have faith to believe this? If you do, then you must live it!

*What saith my Lord unto his servant?* JOSHUA 5:14

Joshua was God's appointed man to lead the people into the new land after the death of Moses. Here we see Joshua falling on his face as he is confronted by a Man but this was no ordinary Man!

What Joshua said and did is noteworthy. Yes, the expectant mother can learn from him, for Joshua asked a good question. Then he was willing to listen to what the Man had to say. Because Joshua asked, listened, and acted in faith, neither arguing nor doubting, we read: "So the Lord was with Joshua;

27

and his fame was noised throughout all the country" (6:27).

Read your Bible, seeking what God has to say to you these waiting days. Then be willing to listen as the Holy Spirit takes the words and makes them meaningful in your experiences. Finally, act, don't argue!

*And the manna ceased . . . ; but they did eat of the fruit of the land . . .* JOSHUA 5:12

Many things happened when the children of Israel entered into the promised land. One of the things was a change in their eating practices, which meant for them a new diet.

Many wonderful things happen in a home awaiting the arrival of a little newcomer. Usually there is more emphasis on sound nutrition when the mother-to-be conscientiously follows her doctor's advice.

"How are 'you' feeling?" This is the question expectant mothers are frequently asked. Happy that woman who can truthfully answer, "Wonderful!" One need only look at the shining light in her happy eyes and see the radiant expression on her face to realize the truth of her answer.

This can be a truly wonderful time for you and other members of the family, especially if good diet practices are followed, greatly contributing to the feeling of good health. The fear of putting on unwanted pounds often leads the mother-to-be to a foolish disregard for what she knows to be healthy eating habits. Not only is she endangering her own health, but—and this would seem to be an even more important consideration—she is assuredly endangering that tiny bit of helplessness entrusted to her care and keeping.

Today reappraise your diet practices. If you have been over-indulging, make this the day for new resolves. If, on the other hand, you have been careless, try to realize anew that the general well-being of our bodies is the result of sound nutrition. This should take on new significance as you face the fact that

28

the health of your unborn child is dependent upon you and your diet right now.

*... choose you this day whom ye will serve; ... but as for me and my house, we will serve the Lord.* JOSHUA 24:15

The most important choice that one must ever make is the same choice that Joshua placed before the people in his final address to them. Clearly he defined for them the alternatives, if they did not choose to serve the Lord. The warning he sounded rings true and clear down through all the years. So, too, does his affirmation that he and his house would serve the Lord.

There are some who, following Joshua's example, have found it necessary to change the direction of their lives completely. I am thinking in particular of the father of a missionary family who took this verse as *his* verse when he first became a Christain. He had been a highly successful businessman, respected and admired in his profession, but within two years after receiving Christ as Saviour *and* Lord of his life, he found himself faced with the full reality of that verse. The choice was not difficult for one who was daily walking with the Lord, and today the man, his wife, and their three children are serving on the mission field in Quito, Ecuador. Great peace of heart and joy unspeakable have followed.

This can be the experience of everyone who chooses to tear down the idols that stand in the way of complete surrender. Such idols as money, fame, and the things only the world can offer never give abiding peace or lasting happiness.

Pray today that you and your house will always make the right choices.

*And the children of Israel did evil in the sight of the Lord ...* JUDGES 2:11

This is a phrase that appears repeatedly in the Book of Judges. Careful study shows a familiar pattern of sinning, suffering, supplication, and salvation. When in their distress the people cried to God, judges were raised up to help deliver them. It is an altogether too-familiar pattern among God's people. One wonders at the continuing mercy of God!

The sin of the children of Israel was one of forgetting—forgetting God. What needless suffering they brought upon themselves because they forgot the Lord! Today read Psalm 103 and marvel with the Psalmist at God's mercy.

*. . . teach us what we shall do unto the child that shall be born.* JUDGES 13:8

God didn't send angels to tell me when I was going to have my babies. I don't imagine He sent angels to you, either! But He did send an angelic messenger to Manoah and his wife, who became the parents of Samson.

So great was Manoah's concern over the fact that they were to become parents, that he intreated—that is, he pleaded—with the Lord to send the man of God again so that they could be taught what to do for the child.

Manoah's plea is one that every prospective father and mother should make their own . . . "teach us what we shall do unto the child that shall be born." How absolutely beautiful! God grant that the beauty, the depth, and the sincerity of this plea shall become lodged in your thinking as you await the child who shall be born to you.

*So Boaz took Ruth, and she was his wife: . . . the Lord gave her conception, and she bare a son.* RUTH 4:13

There are so many interesting and lovely things to be said about this moving narrative that one scarcely knows where to begin. Here one reads the most striking example of love for a mother-in-law that has ever been written. Here one is first introduced to the little village of Bethlehem that is to become the cradle for salvation through One who will trace His genealogy back to Boaz and Ruth. Here we meet the ancestress of our Lord and discover in Ruth such beauty of character that we pause with respectful awe. Here, too, we find in the noble Boaz something of the manliness that every woman looks for and hopes to find in the man of her choice.

G. Campbell Morgan emphasizes the poetic, stately simplicity of one of the closing sentences of this book (4:17): "They called his name Obed: he is the father of Jesse, the father of David."

When the Lord gives to us conception, as He did for Ruth, we have no way of knowing what the future holds for our child. Did Ruth know her child was to be given a place in the historical line of the Saviour of the world? Do you know what your unborn child's tomorrows will hold? Ponder these truths.

*I have asked him of the Lord.* I SAMUEL 1:20

Hannah was not the first, nor was she the last to ask the Lord for a child. We often think of Hannah as the praying mother; her prayers did not end when God remembered and answered her deepest-spoken longings. I am sure the prayers of Hannah followed her son Samuel all his life and influenced him greatly.

We think of Hannah also as the mother who lovingly and patiently stitched a new little coat for her son each year. We remember how, after he was weaned and still a mere child, she presented him to the Lord and brought him to the sanctuary where, under Eli's priestly ministry, the boy served and grew before the Lord.

These are the days when you may be lovingly preparing the little things your new baby will need. As you do this, remember Hannah. "For this child I prayed; and the Lord hath given me my petition which I asked of him" (v. 27). The saintly Hannah is deserving of recognition. She serves as a good example of a woman of prayer for the expectant mother. Read this marvelous story in the first few chapters of I Samuel.

*. . . by him actions are weighed.* I SAMUEL 2:3

This simple, trusting woman confronts us with a truth profound in meaning. Hannah's song in thankfulness sounds a note of triumph that is at once uplifting. Every statement she makes is rich, rich in meaning! We find ourselves joyously thankful for Hannah's thankfulness!

The writer of Proverbs has phrased these same thoughts in this way: "All the ways of a man are clean in his own eyes; but the Lord weigheth the spirits" (16:2). Surely the implications of these truths need little commentary.

Let us pray that our actions are pleasing to the Lord. Let us ask God to motivate our actions, even as He did those of dear Hannah.

*. . . the word of the Lord was precious in those days . . .*
I SAMUEL 3:1

To read these words is to feel the impact of something that is very relevant to the times in which we live. The Word of the Lord was precious in those days; the Word is precious today; but we find ourselves feeling that it is so only to precious few!

How precious is the Word to you today? Precious enough to take the time to read and study? Precious enough to give to others? Precious enough to practice? Precious enough to memorize?

These are precious days for you. Let His Word to you be a part of the preciousness!

*And Samuel grew, and the Lord was with him . . .*
I SAMUEL 3:19

Parents desire many things for their children. Those desires begin to form even before the child is born. Often we hope for them some of the things and experiences which we ourselves never had. Sometimes this can have adverse effects.

Hannah, too, had plans for her son. What strength of character she must have had! After wanting and waiting for a child for so long, she secluded him in the Temple courts for at least twenty years. But Hannah's greatest desire for her child was that he might be devoted to the service of God. What will you desire most of all for your child?

In early boyhood, Samuel received a supernatural call from God. Because he recognized it and was obedient, the Bible tells us, Samuel grew and matured, and the Lord was with him.

Let this be your earnest prayer and heartfelt desire, that your child will early sense the call of God for his love and devotion, and that the response will be willing obedience. Then you will have the same confidence Hannah possessed, that the Lord will always be with your child. What more could any mother ask!

*The Lord that delivered me out of the paw of the lion, and out of the paw of the bear, he will deliver me out of the hand of this Philistine.* I SAMUEL 17:37

In the very first recorded conversation of David, there is a recognition of the greatness of the Lord. How bravely, how fearlessly, David demonstrates his consciousness of the strength of God! Without armor for protection, without weapons, the young lad set out to fight the giant Goliath.

As I, in my thinking, see the scene, I see a parallel. I see brave young fathers and mothers setting out on the new venture of parenthood. I see giants in the form of fear and uncertainty gripping at their hearts. New burdens of financial responsibility, inexperience, and other forces contrive to undermine and destroy their faith. But I also can see that David's Deliverer will act on their behalf when they face the giants, demonstrating their awareness of God's overcoming power.

33

*. . . the soul of Jonathan was knit with the soul of David, and Jonathan loved him as his own soul.* I SAMUEL 18:1

There are many kinds of friends, and friendship is a wonderful thing. Volumes have been written extoling the beauties of friends and friendship, but in this verse we see the beginning of what might well be called one of the most perfect stories of friendship ever recorded.

To show his great love for David, Jonathan gave of himself. It is as we give expression to our feelings—whether by word or deed, or both—that we show our friends that we love them and value their friendship.

Have you shared with your friends the joys you are experiencing in these waiting days? How long has it been since you gave of yourself—a telephone call, a letter, a visit, a home-baked delicacy, the loan of a favorite book—to show that you love your friend?

Today share with a friend the joy and some of the thoughts you are having these days while you look forward with great anticipation to your baby's arrival.


*. . . the Lord struck the child that Uriah's wife bare unto David, and it was very sick.* II SAMUEL 12:15

Read the preceding chapters to obtain the complete picture of the events that led up to the birth of David's and Bathsheba's son. The Prophet Nathan had said the child would die. The child was born; it did become sick, and died.

David's acknowledgment of his sin was genuine. We have no right to stand in judgment of him. The Bible tells us the Lord put away David's sin; nevertheless the Lord did execute a punishment: the child died.

David accepted with yielded heart all that happened. His first act after the child's death was to worship; true repentance showed itself in his attitude in the face of tragedy.

We can learn from David's experience that, even in times of deepest despair, we are to be steadfast, knowing that God doeth all things well. Let us not question God's judgments; but rather let us thank Him for the attitude of David that serves as an example for us. This is how we can meet the testings of life.

*Behold, my son, which came forth of my bowels, seeketh my life . . .* II SAMUEL 16:11

Could anything be more grievous than to have a son or daughter you love turn upon you, even to the point of seeking to kill you? This was King David's experience.

The sorrows of David were many. Polygamy (having several wives at one time) was common in Old Testament days. David's eight wives (as recorded) no doubt complicated things and added to his problem. The humiliation and shame he often endured would have crushed a man with little confidence in God. We begin to understand why he was called "a man after God's own heart."

Discipline of our children is an absolute essential for their present and ultimate well-being; it is essential to our own peace and harmony, too. Become familiar with what the Bible has to say on this subject; study the Proverbs, in particular. It would be well also to equip yourself with other reading material on the subject of behavior (and misbehavior) of children. Your doctor can also make suggestions.

*O my son Absalom, my son, my son Absalom! would God I had died for thee, O Absalom, my son, my son!*

II SAMUEL 18:33

Pathetic! Tragic! How can one really describe the heart-rending lament of David? Five times he repeats the words "my son." Morgan described it movingly: "The deepest cry escaping from David's heart was, 'Would God I had died for thee.' Here David surely reached the profoundest moment of his suffering. We cannot stand in the presence of that suffering without learning the solemn lessons of parental responsibility it has to teach, not merely in training our children, but in that earlier training of ourselves for their sakes."

To give way to one's grief is not to admit weakness. To give expression to our sorrow, even as David did, is a balm for healing. It is only as we let our grief drive us to total despair from which we do not rise, that we show sinful weakness.

How teachable are you? If you are willing to be taught, the suffering of David as a parent can, indeed, as Morgan suggests, teach you much. Today read II Samuel 22.

*When the time of David's death came near, he advised his son Solomon: "I am about to die. You must be strong and behave as a man. You must observe the charge of the Lord your God . . ."* I KINGS 2:1–3, BERKELEY.

It was the pleas of Solomon's mother that resulted in Solomon becoming heir to his father's throne. The responsibilities that loomed upon the horizon for Solomon must have appeared ominous at that moment. We see his father David on his deathbed, reminding his son that the only safe way in life is the path that leads to God.

We can be sure David's last remarks were no weak utterances; they were issued from a heart that had known much of bitter experience. His charge to Solomon is a fitting reminder that all of life should be lived so that death's beckonings will find us ready.

There is a familiar Christian motto, "Prepare to meet thy God," which involves a daily preparation. Ask God to meet your weaknesses and to supply strength that will enable you to live before your family as an example worthy of your children.

*Give therefore thy servant an understanding heart to judge thy people, that I may discern between good and bad: for who is able to judge . . . so great a people?* I KINGS 3:9

36

How wonderful it is to experience answered prayer! This was Solomon's experience.

Solomon was the wisest man who ever lived (I Kings 4:29–34). In spite of his great wisdom as a leader, he failed tragically in many respects. His prayer at this point, the very outset of his reign as king, stands unmatched as an acknowledgment of great personal need. God had said, "Ask what I shall give thee" (I Kings 3:5). Solomon made the wisest choice possible; the prayer pleased the Lord.

If there is any prayer which I, as a mother, have uttered with great frequency, it is the appeal for patience and understanding. Parents have need of the very thing Solomon requested; the situations into which we are thrust from the moment our children make their entrance into the world calls for wisdom from on high. Without it, we fail miserably.

In the Sermon on the Mount, Christ exhorts us to pray: "Ask, and it shall be given you; seek, and ye shall find; knock, and it shall be opened unto you" (Matthew 7:7).

Ask wisely, as Solomon did, and you too will experience answered prayer.

*Give her the living child, and in no wise slay it: she is the mother thereof.* I KINGS 3:27

Suffocation, a terrible accident, had claimed the life of an infant, and King Solomon was called upon to exercise a judgment. Two women had given birth to babies. One mother had laid on her child in the night, suffocating it. Upon arising and making the horrifying discovery, she took the other woman's baby, sleeping nearby, and left her own dead son in its place.

Solomon's judgment (vv. 24–25) showed the wisdom of God that was in him as he administered true justice. The motherly compassion of the child's rightful mother went out to him as she declared her willingness to let the other woman keep her child rather than have it slain.

Compassion such as you have never felt before will be your experience as you at last hold in your arms His precious gift, your heritage of the Lord.

*King Solomon had Hiram brought from Tyre. He was the son of a widow. . . . He was intelligent, talented, and skilled . . .*
I KINGS 7:13–14, BERKELEY

Attempts were made in Biblical times to protect widows from injustice and exploitation. The Bible abounds with references showing the kindness and consideration accorded to the fatherless and the widowed. Such humane treatment was part of the Hebrews' belief that, in their kindness to widows and those less fortunate members of society, they were, in effect, carrying out God's will.

Solomon engaged the highly skilled Hiram, son of a widow, to do all of the brass work in the Temple. As one reads about his workmanship, one is amazed at the magnificent proportions and lavish descriptions. Certainly the father of Hiram, in whose trade the son followed, had taught his son well before he died.

Having grown up as a fatherless child, my appreciation for the references to the widow and her children are especially keen. Look up the following verses and then evaluate your own attitude, in the light of the Word, toward those who are fatherless, motherless, or widowed: Exodus 22:22; Deuteronomy 10:17–18; 14:23, 29; II Kings 4:1–8; Isaiah 1:17; Isaiah 10:1–2; Job 29:15–16; Job 31:16–22; Psalm 146:9; Mark 12:41–44; I Timothy 5:3–16.

*But King Solomon loved many strange women, . . . and his wives turned away his heart.* I KINGS 11:1, 3

What a sad commentary on wives! It was the practice of polygamy that was Solomon's undoing. Imagine trying to keep seven hundred wives and three hundred concubines happy!

Material magnificence distracted Solomon as he succumbed

to the pressure of his wives' pleadings and built temples to their heathen gods. In the first nine verses of this chapter we read six times a reference to the fact that Solomon turned away his heart from God. ". . . the Lord was angry with Solomon . . ." (v. 9), and God's judgment fell upon him.

Solomon's experiences stand as a holy warning that we must keep our hearts right before God if we are to know His pleasure. Pray that you may be the kind of wife and mother who will encourage her husband and family to keep their hearts fixed on the Lord.

*Rehoboam the son of Solomon reigned in Judah. . . . And Judah did evil in the sight of the Lord.* I KINGS 14:21-22

We need not be surprised when we read of the deterioration of the kingdoms of Judah and Israel in our Bible. The sons of Solomon had heathen mothers!

Surely these Old Testament stories remind us frequently of the folly of sin. The weight of influence in keeping a child on the path of good conduct lies within the home. This is not something we can relegate to the church, school, or community. Though their influence is felt, the responsibility remains first and foremost ours.

*And the word of the Lord came unto him . . .* I KINGS 17:2

The Prophet Elijah now comes across the Biblical landscape. His appearance is sudden, and he brings with him the Word of the Lord. Elijah's unquestioning obedience to the Lord, and his subsequent actions, is remarkable. The manner in which God provides his nourishment and protection is most unusual. No stress is laid upon his nationality; we do not know who his parents were. Ravens fed him. God's Word is with him; and God uses him.

As God's Word comes to you these days, draw near to Him, and His provision for you will be as "raven's food."

*And Elijah took the child, . . . and delivered him unto his mother . . .* I KINGS 17:23

When drought and famine came, the brook from which Elijah drank dried up. The Lord directed him to the Zarephath widow, where he was sustained. Miraculously God provided a continuing supply of food for the widow, Elijah, and the widow's son.

Then tragedy struck: the child fell sick and died. Elijah's cry to the Lord, ". . . let this child's soul come into him again" (v. 21), did not go unanswered. When Elijah gave the child back to his mother, the woman said, "Now by this I know that thou art a man of God, and that the word of the Lord in thy mouth is truth" (v. 24).

Let this be a word of assurance to your heart. The God of Elijah is your God, and His concern for His children never changes.

*I will not bring the evil in his days: but in his son's days will I bring the evil upon his house.* I KINGS 21:29

Walt Whitman wrote:

### There Was a Child Went Forth

There was a child went forth every day;
And the first object he look'd upon, that object he
  became;
And that object became part of him for the day, or a
  certain part of the day, or for many years, or
  stretching cycles of years . . .
These became part of that child who went forth every
  day, and who now goes, and will always go forth
  every day.

Surely Ahab's son, who succeeded his father to the throne, was a man steeped in the ways of idolatry. The things Ahaziah looked upon as a child, and the influence of his evil parents,

40

had a marked effect upon him. His mother was the wicked Jezebel.

God's pronouncements, recorded Biblical history, and the poet's words make the expectant mother aware of the influence she will exert for good or bad upon her children.

*And his mother's name was . . .*
I AND II KINGS; I AND II CHRONICLES
This phrase appears with regularity in the books of the Bible that record the history of the Kings. If these mothers could have known that history would so unerringly record their part in shaping the lives of their sons as rulers, would they have lived differently?

We read of fifteen rulers of Judah from the southern kingdom. Of these, seven did "good" or "right" in the sight of the Lord; the other eight did "evil." The emphasis is placed upon the role of their mothers.

When we read that these kings walked in the ways of their fathers and in the ways of their mothers, let us thank God that we are living on this side of Bible history, where we can benefit from what we read.

*Go, . . . and live thou and thy children . . .*   II KINGS 4:7
As one goes through the Bible, searching for those statements and stories that speak particularly of children, mothers, and fathers, it is illuminating to find the thread of consistency that shows God's constant concern for children. His Father-love shows itself many times in His dealings with them through His prophets.

The miracles which the prophet Elisha performed were deeds of kindness and mercy. In this particular instance the debt-ridden widow who appealed to Elisha for help received in abundance enough to pay her debts and to provide a living for her and her children.

In the Sermon on the Mount, our Lord speaks a truth that

41

reminds us of this widow. "Give and men will give to you—yes, good measure, pressed down, shaken together and running over will they pour into your lap. For whatever measure you use with other people, they will use in their dealings with you" (Luke 6:38, PHILLIPS).

*About this season, according to the time of life, thou shalt embrace a son.* II KINGS 4:16

A miraculous thing occurred in the village of Shunem. Elisha was befriended by a couple who had no children, and because of their great kindness to him, he wanted to do something for them. He sent his servant with a request something like this: "Look, since you have exercised all this painstaking care for us, what can be done for you?"

The woman's husband was old, and, humanly speaking, it would have been impossible for the couple to have children. But with God all things are possible, and the woman gave birth to a son the next season, as Elisha had said.

Joy, as only a mother who has just given birth to a child can experience, filled the Shunemite woman's heart. As you embrace your newborn child for the very first time, you will feel the same overwhelming sense of gratitude and aching tenderness that engulfed that woman's being.

*She is in deep anxiety ...* II KINGS 4:27 BERKELEY

Elisha correctly sensed the Shunemite woman's anxiety. She showed great faith in seeking the prophet's help as her child lay sick unto death. When Elisha arrived at the home, the child was dead. Again we see a miracle take place as God, through the prophet, restores the child to life.

The day of miracles is not over. It is only as we lose contact with God through our failure to seek Him in prayer, and through His Word, that we deny ourselves His power. Avail yourself of the miracle of His transforming love, and experience a renewal of power to live the victorious Christian life through Christ. Anxious moments as a parent will still befall you; but in His strength miracles can happen, and you will find the anxious time bearable.

*Seven years old was Jehoash when he began to reign.*

II KINGS 11:21

It was the terrible wrath of a mother that resulted in a wholesale slaughter of innocent people who, as part of the royal family, were destined to ascend the throne. One son was successfully abducted and saved. The child, one year old at the time, was concealed with his nurse for six long years.

Seven is a very tender age. A seven-year-old today would usually be a second-grader, requiring much instruction and guidance. It was because of Jehoiada, a priest, that seven-year-old Jehoash did what was right, for he was well instructed by this man of God.

One cannot understand how any mother could order the massacre of members of her own family. Again we see the influence of the mother, for Athaliah who destroyed the royal offspring had as her own mother the wicked Jezebel.

*... they caused their sons and their daughters to pass through the fire ...* II KINGS 17:17

A casual reading of this verse does not tell us much. But stark horror confronts us as we discover that this describes the worship of Moloch. It was the most brutal and corrupt of all pagan rites, requiring the sacrifice of children.

Moloch was represented as a huge animal with human head and arms. A fire was lit inside the idol and the children were placed in its arms. It is only when we realize that these people forsook God that we can comprehend how anything as horrible as human sacrifice—and children at that—could take place.

43

Today thank God for His love which fills your heart and passes all understanding. Read Psalm 106 in its entirety.

*And the Lord was with him; and he prospered whithersoever he went forth.* II KINGS 18:7

The reign of Hezekiah was characterized by the good he did. The influence of the godly Prophet Isaiah was felt throughout this kingship. Hezekiah relied heavily upon his old and trusted friend, Isaiah, who prayed and advised him. We read that Hezekiah trusted in the Lord, that he clave to the Lord, that he did not depart from following Him, and because of this the Lord was with him.

Hezekiah had an evil father; if it had not been for the wise counsel of Isaiah he might have turned out quite differently. His life speaks to us of the importance of the right guidance, spiritual nourishment, and good leadership in the lives of children.

How careful we are in the preparation of our infant's formula and food. The vitamin bottle is kept near at hand. Even so, we need to be sure we are not neglecting spiritual nourishment for our own inner well-being. The future welfare of our children will be dependent upon the teachings they receive at our knees.

*What have they seen in thine house?* II KINGS 20:15

When the Babylonian king went to see Hezekiah, he was shown all of the precious things in the house and dominion. When Isaiah went to see Hezekiah, he asked a searching question: "What have they seen in thine house?" It was a good question. It is a very relevant one for the times in which we live, when so much stress is laid upon what is seen in our homes.

A neighbor calls the furniture in her house Contemptuous, not Contemporary. In reply I told her ours was Early Matrimonial, not Early American! What we sit, walk, sleep, and eat on is really unimportant. The household treasures, such as they are, that are seen in our homes are not nearly as important as other influences that make for happy living.

Isaiah had a prophetic word of warning for Hezekiah: "Behold, the days come, that all that is in thine house, and that which thy fathers have laid up in store unto this day, shall be carried into Babylon: nothing shall be left, saith the Lord. And of thy sons that shall issue from thee, which thou shalt beget, shall they take away; and they shall be eunuchs in the palace of the king of Babylon" (vv. 17–18). The prophecy was fulfilled.

The warning remains a solemn reminder that the things of this life do pass away and perish. Earlier Isaiah had said, "Set thine house in order; for thou shalt die . . ." (v. 1). He wasn't speaking about material concerns!

*Because thine heart was tender . . .* II KINGS 22:19

The story of Josiah, the king who ascended the throne when he was eight years old, is a favorite story with Sunday-school-age children.

The Temple was in a terrible state of disrepair, and buried in the rubble the Book of the Law was found. With sensitive soul, Josiah consulted with the scribe, the priest, and Huldah the Prophetess regarding the meaning of the words of the Book.

The Word of the Lord that came to Josiah was one of encouragement. It was because of the tenderness of his heart, his loyalty, and his penitent attitude that Josiah would see a reformation in the land and be allowed to go to his grave in peace at the close of his life.

The tenderheartedness of Josiah is a virtue parents should pray will be found in their offspring. To be sensitive to evil, to have a conscience quick to discern between right and wrong—these are qualities of the heart that is tender.

In your own heart decide now that you will endeavor to

instill tenderness into the heart of your child, even while his years are tender.

### *And the sons of ...*  I CHRONICLES

A most remarkable genealogical record is set before us in the Book of I Chronicles. Beginning with the first man, Adam, the chronicler traces the multiplication of people, showing the movement of the hand of God in the history of mankind.

No doubt you will come into possession of a "baby" book as a gift. If not, be sure you obtain one; you will enjoy keeping a record of the "firsts" in your child's life, and there are many other things such a book will enable you to note. Included among the pages of a "baby" book you will usually find a "family tree" section. You will need the help of parents and grandparents to fill this out accurately. (We have the signatures of the progenitors in some of the spaces in our childrens' books. With some of them now in heaven, the record seems even more meaningful.)

Just as the Bible genealogies were useful, and have since proved of immeasurable worth, to the Bible student—especially as they show the Messianic line—a genealogy can be of real interest to every family through the years. This may be a project you can begin now in your "waiting" days.

### *... the genealogy is not to be reckoned after the birthright.*
I CHRONICLES 5:1

Names make news. How true! Ezra, who is generally regarded as the author of the Chronicles, found this to be true in his day also. Two names in particular stand out as we view the record in Chapter 5, Reuben and Joseph.

Reuben stands out as a sinning son; but Joseph, his brother, was the one to whom the birthright was given. Joseph was God's own choice. Here we see a principle of divine selection at work as sin and disobedience are ruled out in favor of infinite justice.

God's all-seeing eye will always overrule in the affairs of men and nations. Joseph is an example of a young man who served the nation of Israel with determined valor. His was a godly heritage.

The most important heritage you can bequeath your children will be godliness. Paul wrote, ". . . lead a quiet and peaceable life in all godliness and honesty. For this is good and acceptable in the sight of God our Saviour." (I Timothy 2:2–3).

*Who am I, O Lord God, and what is mine house, that thou hast brought me hitherto?* I CHRONICLES 17:16

The thought came to David that the Ark of the Covenant of the Lord belonged in something better than a tent (v. 1). From that moment on it became his burning desire to make preparations so that, after his death, Solomon, his son, could build a magnificent Temple (I Chronicles 22:5–6). Through these days of preparation David found himself crying, "Who am I, O Lord God . . . ?"

The expectant mother, feeling the new life stir within her, sensing the immensity of the call which God has extended to her—motherhood—finds herself echoing the cry, "Who am I, O Lord God . . . ?"

Today read John 15. Let the realization that God has chosen you (v. 16) to bear witness to Him sweep over you. Then, too, for the special privilege of motherhood you have also been chosen. Who are you? You are His own. He loves you. Your love in return—for Him, for your family, and for others —is the response He desires of you as a fruit-bearing Christian.

*For ye are all the children of God by faith in Christ Jesus.*
*For as many of you as have been baptized into Christ have*
*put on Christ. There is neither Jew nor Greek, there is neither*
*bond nor free, there is neither male nor female: for ye are*

*all one in Christ Jesus. And if ye be Christ's, then are ye
Abraham's seed, and heirs according to the promise.*

GALATIANS 3:26-29

### In Christ Is Neither Greek Nor Jew

Test me God and try me sorely,
See if I am fit to do
This great work Thou hast to offer
Trusting Thee to see me through.

Help me always to remember
Thou hast made us one and all;
Thou are not willing one should perish,
Thy Spirit grieves if one dost fall.

Then use me, pray, to bear the message
Of the Master's saving grace,
For every soul Thou hast created—
Dare we mention color, race?

We are all of one great family,
Those He ransomed from the fall;
May each heart and knee bow humbly
To the Father of us all.

NAOMI CARR LANCE

*Behold, a son shall be born to thee . . .* I CHRONICLES 22:9
Before Solomon was born, David knew that this child would
be a son. This sometimes happened in Biblical times; the ele-
ment of surprise as to the child's sex was often missing. Of
course, the greatest honor that could come to a woman was to
give birth to a son.

I know of no one who knew, before giving birth, that her
child would be a boy or a girl. My doctor may have ventured

a few guesses based on a certain number of heartbeats and his previous experience, but at best they were just that—guesses.

You may be hoping for a son—or a daughter. You may have very high hopes. Are you going to be prepared for the opposite of your hopes? Suppose a son arrives, instead of the little daughter you want so badly? How will you react?

I'd like to share with you something that happened when our fourth baby was born. When Mommy and baby arrived home from the hospital, to be enthusiastically greeted by older brother and two big sisters, my older daughter said, "Oh, Mom, I'm so thankful! I prayed for a blond baby—for a boy —and that's just what we got!" The tenderness in her voice and the sweet look on her face added meaning to her words. It was time for Mommy to pose a question, a serious question: "But suppose we hadn't been given a blond baby boy?" Tonia thought seriously for a moment, looked at the precious little bundle in Mommy's arms, and replied with touching ten-year-old insight, "Well, then, God would have said 'No.'"

*Be ye strong therefore, and let not your hands be weak: for your work shall be rewarded.* II CHRONICLES 15:7

Under King Asa the nation was purged of its idols, its enemies were overthrown, and drastic reform measures swept across the land. Then came the time when Asa's courage began to fail. It was at that precise moment when a man anointed with the Spirit of God appeared to the king, offering words of wisdom: "The Lord is with you, while ye be with him; and if ye seek him, he will be found of you; but if ye forsake him, he will forsake you" (v. 2).

With renewed courage Asa continued to act, even to the point of removing his own mother from the queen's throne. His reason? She had made a repulsive Asherah image to worship. Asherahs were wooden poles or tree trunks dedicated to the worship of the nature goddess, Astarte. On one pole, or stump, the likeness of the female secret organ was carved, and on another that of the male; a Baal altar was set between the two. Not content merely to depose his mother, Asa cut down her idol, stamped on it, and burned it.

There are days when the pregnant woman finds her strength, as it were, ebbing. The added weight, the pressure, the strain on the back, the tired muscles, aching limbs, veins in the legs —all these things may contribute to a general feeling of weakness and inability to cope with the demands of the day. Let the word-tonic, as given to Asa, renew your strength: "Be ye strong therefore. . . ."

*For the eyes of the Lord run to and fro throughout the whole earth, to shew himself strong in the behalf of them whose heart is perfect toward him.* II CHRONICLES 16:9

This is a sad chapter in the life of Asa, but you would do well to read it in its entirety. Here we see the king so engrossed with the problems of war and his own physical suffering that he does not even seek the Lord's help. It is really sad when a person strays so far that he will not listen to those who wisely and lovingly offer counsel.

God is always willing to offer His strength on behalf of one whose heart is full of integrity toward Him. There are times in the lives of all of us when it seems that our hearts will surely fail within us. That is when we need to make certain our hearts are fixed on Him, or herein lies our failure and uncertainty.

You will need His strength. Praise Him today for His watchful eye over you, for guarding you and the child 'neath your heart.

*. . . all Judah stood before the Lord, with their little ones, their wives, and their children.* II CHRONICLES 20:13

A huge array of the enemy was making its way toward the inhabitants of Judah. Great fear gripped at the hearts of the

50

people and they were at a loss to know what to do. A fast was proclaimed and the people were called together to ask help of the Lord. We see King Jehoshaphat standing in the congregation in the Temple, praying. He concludes his plea for the overthrow of the enemy by declaring, ". . . but our eyes are upon thee" (v. 12).

This is a touching picture, this king surrounded by his people. We can envision little children hanging on their mothers' skirts; mothers with babes in their arms; little boys regarding with awe the serious expressions on the faces of their fathers; fathers with their arms across the shoulders of their wives in a comforting, reassuring gesture. On such a scene the Spirit of the Lord descended and spoke through a man called Jahaziel: "Be not afraid nor dismayed . . . ; for the battle is not yours, but God's" (v. 15).

There isn't a single battle you or your children need to fear. Regardless of outward circumstances, God is greater than the most dreaded foe. We need to teach our children this marvelous truth, and to show them from the Word that it is God who will fight against our enemies.

*. . . his mother was his counsellor to do wickedly.*

II CHRONICLES 22:3

Of all the Biblical statements about mothers, this verse leaps out with such an impact that it strikes one with disbelief. Imagine a mother deliberately counseling her child to do wickedly! But this mother did.

Mothers are many things to their families. Someone has suggested that the average mother simultaneously conducts a university, a clothing establishment, a laundry, a restaurant; and at the same time she is a police, health, and truant officer. Add to this the financial problems she shares with her husband, and the multitudinous other tasks and responsibilities, and a picture emerges of the greatness of motherhood.

An imposing list could surely be drawn of what is expected

of us as mothers. Topping such a list might well be the responsibility of counseling. Counseling involves giving advice, and through the years you will be counseling your child in all kinds of situations and circumstances.

Even as this book was being written, our oldest son needed special counseling. We had an interesting and mutually satisfying counseling session, but the precedent for this began years ago when he was in his crib. You are surprised at that? Proper discipline and training of the child begins in infancy; your job as counselor begins the moment you give birth.

*The fathers shall not die for the children, neither shall the children die for the fathers, but every man shall die for his own sin.* II CHRONICLES 25:4

A king was executing justice; his father had been murdered, and punishment of the murderers was necessary. He was acting in accordance with the Law of Moses.

A truth has been uttered which stands through all generations. There are many fathers—mothers, too—who have died for their children, sacrificing their own lives to spare their offspring in times of disaster. The love of parents for their children is such that in moments of crisis we would die that they might live. Such sacrifice would be in vain if our children did not live Christ-honoring lives.

Salvation is a personal thing. We experience it only as we acknowledge our sinfulness and seek His forgiveness: "For he hath made him to be sin for us, who knew no sin; that we might be made the righteousness of God in him" (II Corinthians 5:21).

We begin early in our children's lives to teach them about Jesus. From their first faltering tries as they lisp the name of Jesus, to the day when they place their trust in Him, and even ever after, we instill truth and endeavor to lead them in the right way.

52

*. . . seek . . . a right way for us, and for our little ones . . .*

EZRA 8:21

A trip is in progress, a long, perilous trip. Ezra, the priest, is leading a host of people to Jerusalem. Before them lie seven hundred miles of hot desert country. Enemies lie in wait along the way.

How different things are today! A long trip finds us readying ourselves in ways far different from those of the ancient peoples. But there should be one similarity. Do we humble ourselves before God, seeking the right way for ourselves and our little ones?

We shall not forget the first long trip we took as a family. We took a train to Colorado when our little one was four, and before we left home we paused around the kitchen table and sought God's traveling mercies. The words of a precious little girl, spoken with sweet, trusting simplicity, have stayed with us: "God, come with us. We're going to have such a good time!"

We need to seek the right way for ourselves and our little ones whether we are at home or going away. Entreat God, even as Ezra did, for this guidance in all the days that lie ahead.

*So . . .* NEHEMIAH

In the book that bears his name we meet Nehemiah the patriot, statesman, and reformer. He may have been a man of few words; at any rate, the two-letter word *so* occurs thirty-two times. He is remembered as the man used mightily by God to rebuild the wall surrounding Jerusalem. We see in him a man of prayer, action, and courage in the face of persecution and ridicule (2:19; 4:17–18).

Did the mother of Nehemiah realize the great potential of her son when she lovingly ministered to his needs as a child? Did the mother of Martin Luther know that she was rocking the Reformation in her cradle?

I once overheard a young mother complaining bitterly that

53

she felt as though she were living in an intellectual vacuum. We may frown disapprovingly, raise our eyebrows, and think, "What kind of a mother would say that!" And, yet, I wonder if other mothers come close to thinking something similar at times, even though it isn't put into words. When we have wiped up spilled milk for the umpteenth time, tackled a huge stack of ironing, and spent the greater share of a day washing and waxing floors, not to mention the dirty diapers that are always accumulating, we may feel as though we too were living in an intellectual vacuum.

The Christian wife and mother can rise above the monotony and seeming drudgery of the everyday tasks. She recognizes that hers is a bountiful ministry. Today many modern women are turning their hearts from the demands of motherhood. To do so is to turn from a woman's most sublime throne. The small acts of kindness, the favorite home-baked treat, tucking the bed covers in place—all of the things we do are opportunities to build Christianity into the very structure of the lives of our children.

Nehemiah's "so" says something to me; it speaks of a man confronted with gigantic responsibilities. But he accomplished the work to which he was called, and with meekness and humility. He did not elaborate or complain, but simply said, "So. . . ." Such an attitude of mind and accompanying faithfulness are needed if you and I are to be the kind of mothers counted worthy.

*He was foster father to . . . Esther, his uncle's daughter; because she had neither father nor mother living.*

ESTHER 2:7, BERKELEY

The cousin who became foster father could not know that the child he adopted and brought up with a fatherly devotion would someday repay his tender love with a heroic love of her own. Mordecai was but one of the Jews living in Persia who

had been carried away from Jerusalem in the Babylonian captivity.

As Esther matured in the ways of women she was described as having a lovely form and features. God endowed her with a radiant beauty for a very special reason.

Mordecai lived and worked in the palace of King Ahasuerus. One day the king decided to host a party that would last one hundred and eighty days. Guests from all the provinces of the Persians and the Medes arrived, and the party turned into a drunken orgy. With too much wine under his belt, the king ordered Vashti the queen to appear to display her beauty.

The customs of those days seem so alien to our ways that one finds it difficult at times to like what one reads. The manner in which Esther became a part of the King's harem is an example.

Read the book of Esther and be thankful you are living in a place and time where women are not regarded as mere playthings for men.

*And the king loved Esther above all the women, and she obtained grace and favour in his sight more than all the virgins; so that he set the royal crown upon her head, and made her queen instead of Vashti.* ESTHER 2:17

Persian wives did not disobey their husbands; but on the other hand, neither did they make public appearances. Queen Vashti found herself in a terrible predicament; loyalty to womanhood, not her husband, cost her a throne and a husband. Because of her refusal to appear before the king's guests, she caused her husband great embarrassment, and for that she was dethroned.

It was thus that Esther found herself in a beauty parade, as it were, that resulted in her becoming queen in Vashti's place. We may not like the events that led to her becoming queen, but we must recognize the hand of God at work in placing her in such a providential position.

We feel a womanly sympathy toward Vashti; but God can

use evil for good, and this He accomplished through the lovely Esther. An adopted child became the saviour of her people in a peculiar sense. God's divine purpose cannot be thwarted; only He knows the end from the beginning. Even the faint stirrings of life within you are predestined by God. We, too, and our children, have been adopted—adopted by God!

"Long ago before He made the world God chose us to be His very own, through what Christ would do for us; He decided then to make us holy in His eyes, without a single fault —we who stand before Him covered with His love. His unchanging plan has always been to adopt us into His own family by sending Jesus Christ to die for us. And He did this because He wanted to!" (Ephesians 1:4–5, LIVING LETTERS).

*. . . who knoweth whether thou art come to the kingdom for such a time as this?* ESTHER 4:14

A wicked plot designed to exterminate the Jews scattered throughout the kingdom was hatched by a man with much authority. Esther's husband, the king, signed the orders, sealing them with his ring. "And the letters were sent . . . to destroy, to kill, and to cause to perish, all Jews, both young and old, little children and women . . ." (3:13).

Esther appealed to her husband's manliness. Standing before him in all her beauty she made a request of him. She asked the king and the wicked Haman to come to a banquet, at which she would make known her petition. It was then that she revealed her true identity, exposing Haman and his evil plot. The words Mordecai had uttered, "Who knows but what you have come to the kingdom for such a time as this?" were choice, as Esther valiantly pleaded her cause. The destiny of a race hung precariously in the balance. God used her to deliver His chosen people.

Yes, in Esther's hand a people's destiny was placed. It did not come in the form of a child; but for you it may. Your hands, God willing, will hold a child divinely destined for a special

56

purpose in Gods' unfolding plan. When God's hand shaped woman, His design included her capacity to bear children. The mother's hand in the child's life is helping to shape God's plan for that life. William Ross Wallace wrote: "The hand that rocks the cradle is the hand that rules the world."

*And there were born unto him seven sons and three daughters.*
JOB 1:2

If you are thinking that one can learn a great deal from the father of ten children, you are right—especially when that father happens to be Job!

There are precious lessons to be gleaned from the Book of Job. We meet him as a godly man, the father of a fine family. He is also introduced to us as a very wealthy man, considered as the greatest of all the men of the East.

Job's holiness, his riches, and his concern for the heart condition of his children stand out as we begin the story of the most severe afflictions ever to befall one man in one day.

Read Job's story and become acquainted with this father. Ask God to reveal much of practical worth to you that will help you to trust Him in known and unknown circumstances.

*Naked came I out of my mother's womb, and naked shall I return thither: the Lord gave, and the Lord hath taken away; blessed be the name of the Lord.* JOB 1:21

G. Campbell Morgan explains the conversation between Satan and God, recorded in this first chapter, as heaven in argument with hell about earth. Satan makes the accusation that Job's attitude toward God is based on pure selfishness; he boasts that if Job were to be denied his possessions, his loyalty to God would cease.

The storm of Satan's power falls upon Job. His oxen, asses, and camels are stolen by bandits; lightning strikes, burning his sheep; his servants are slain. As if this were not bad enough, the roof of the house collapses and kills his children.

Satan, are you watching? Are you listening? Job is mourning, yes; to be sure, he is deeply grieved; but he is also worshiping, and he is speaking. His words are words of wisdom. *Blessed*, not cursed, be the name of the Lord, Satan. Job is still praising God!

Let this sink into our minds to help fortify us against the onslaughts of the adversary.

*Then said his wife unto him, Dost thou still retain thine integrity? curse God, and die. But he said unto her, Thou speakest as one of the foolish women speaketh. What? shall we receive good at the hand of God, and shall we not receive evil?* JOB 2:9–10

Satan is not satisfied. Again he confronts God with the accusation that, because Job's own life has not been touched, he can speak words of praise. Again Satan is allowed to test Job and we see him afflicted with boils from head to foot. Added to this Job's wife counsels him to curse God and die!

The Word declares that in spite of all this, Job did not sin with his lips. Up to this point Job's loyalty stands out as a perfect example of patience in adversity.

Job's wife appears to be lacking in understanding. There are those who point to her as a woman who failed her husband in his time of greatest trouble. There are others who regard her words as misguided sympathy. Regardless of which view one accepts, we can learn from this conversation between husband and wife.

*Why did I not die at birth and expire when I came forth from the womb? Why did the knees receive me, or why the breasts that I should nurse?* JOB 3:11–12, BERKELEY

Do not condemn Job for crying out. For seven days and nights Job's three best friends had been sitting with him in silence, thus showing that they shared his grief and woe. To give expression to deep sorrow was the natural cry of a heart overflowing with agony. There is a solace in tears and weeping that comes in no other way.

The debate between Job and his friends contains great words of wisdom. Job firmly maintains his integrity.

Never forget, as you think of this man, that he was a father who had lost his dearest earthly possessions—his ten children. There is nothing wrong with having a sensitive soul, for with Job one can say, ". . . mine eye poureth out tears unto God" (Job 16:20).

*So the Lord blessed the latter end of Job more than his beginning.* JOB 42:12

Job's prosperity and happiness were restored in greater measure. The greatest blessing that he experienced surely came when he again received from the hand of the Lord seven sons and three daughters. We smile appreciatively as we read that in all the land there were no women as beautiful as Job's daughters. God *is* good!

Have we learned from the experience of Job that we must trust God under unknown circumstances? This may be your first experience of childbirth; or it may be a familiar experience. The conditions that will surround this birth, however, cannot be known until the moment of delivery arrives. Do you have faith in God? Then trust Him implicitly.

*I laid me down and slept; I awaked; for the Lord sustained me.* PSALM 3:5

*My voice shalt thou hear in the morning, O Lord; in the morning will I direct my prayer unto thee, and will look up.*
PSALM 5:3

*. . . commune with your own heart upon your bed, and be still.* PSALM 4:4

These are morning and evening Psalms surely meant to show

the wisdom of seeking the Lord's blessing at the beginning and at the close of each day.

Matthew Henry has shown us, in *The Secret of Communion With God*, that the real secret lies in seeking communion with Him the first thing in the morning, then at noon, and again at night. The Psalmist elsewhere tells us, "Evening, and morning, and at noon, will I pray, and cry aloud: and he shall hear my voice (Psalm 55:17).

A friend once referred to her "clothesline prayers." Her explanation revealed a constant line of communication between her and a prayer-hearing God, even while she hung her children's clothes on the line.

Every mother should establish a quiet time for devotions that include prayer and Bible study. From such moments we draw strength and guidance that leave us renewed in spirit, much better able to cope with the everyday problems and situations of life.

*Out of the mouth of babes and sucklings hast thou ordained strength because of thine enemies, that thou mightest still the enemy and the avenger.* PSALM 8:2

Two things in particular attest to God's glory: nature and man; children, especially, prove God's great love. Jesus Himself quoted this very verse from the Psalm. When the children in the Temple said, "Hosanna to the son of David," the chief priests and scribes were moved with indignation. Then it was that Jesus said, "Hearest thou what these say? . . . Yea; have ye never read, Out of the mouth of babes and sucklings thou hast perfected praise?" (Matthew 21:16).

Some of the happiest memories we have as parents are those times when our little ones sing praises to Jesus. Our hearts rejoice as the two-year-old sings "Jesus, Jesus" at play. Such experiences await the mother-to-be.

Praise Jesus today with your own heart and voice.

*Help, Lord; for the godly man ceaseth; for the faithful fail from among the children of men.* PSALM 12:1

We must remember, as we look at the Psalms, that most of them were written by David during his reign as king. In our meditations we have read of the trials and heartaches David endured. The evil time in which he lived was characterized by the failure of godly men.

As we read this and the other Psalms, we get the feeling that they are so applicable to the day in which we live. The faithful few are still in the minority; the cry, "Help, Lord!" is on our lips, too.

*Thou art He who took me out of the womb, who made me trust when upon my mother's breast. Upon Thee have I been cast from my birth; since my mother bore me, Thou hast been my God.* PSALM 22:9–10, BERKELEY

This is considered "The Psalm of the Cross." It begins with the very same words Christ uttered from the cross: "My God, my God, why hast thou forsaken me?" and ends with the same thought, "It is finished." Charles H. Spurgeon has expressed the view that this Psalm actually may have been repeated by our Lord when He was hanging on the cross.

The beauty of childbirth is seen in the verses chosen for our meditation. The true function of a mother with her child upon her breast is demonstrated. And finally, the fact that from the moment of birth parents can entrust their children to God is set forth.

*Save Thy people, and bless Thy heritage; nourish them and carry them forever.* PSALM 28:9, BERKELEY

*The counsel of the Lord stands for ever, the thoughts of his heart to all generations.* PSALM 33:11

*Come, sons and daughters, listen to me, I will teach you reverence for the Lord.* PSALM 34:11, BERKELEY

The secret of life—the good life—is to be found as we

reverence the Lord. It is only as we seek His ways that we and our children shall find true peace and happiness in life.

*. . . the Lord will command his lovingkindness in the day-time, and in the night his song shall be with me, and my prayer unto the God of my life.* PSALM 42:8

*Fear took hold upon them there, and pain, as of a woman in travail.* PSALM 48:6

That one who is trusting God has the assurance that the Lord's loving-kindness is upon him, day and night. A woman facing childbirth needs this assurance. The first and greatest need of any life is God. How assuring in the travail of labor preceding birth, whether in the daylight hours or in the darkness of night, to know that the God of your life is hearing your prayers and will help you.

*Behold, I was shapen in iniquity; and in sin did my mother conceive me.* PSALM 51:5

Conception within marital bonds is not sin. The Psalmist is here acknowledging the fact of sin, original sin, in the world. Paul put it this way: "Wherefore, as by one man sin entered into the world, and death by sin; and so death passed upon all men, for that all have sinned" (Romans 5:12). Jesus, in speaking to Nicodemus, explained it this way: "That which is born of the flesh is flesh; and that which is born of the Spirit is spirit" (John 3:6).

The precious infant you will hold in your arms will nevertheless have been born in a sinful state. But we commit our children to God and trust His love for children to keep them until that day when they are old enough to understand and make a personal commitment of their own selves. God is love. To this we cling.

*God looked down from heaven upon the children of men, to*

*see if there were any that did understand, that did seek God.*

He is still looking down from heaven upon the children of men. He is going to look down upon your family also. Will they understand? Will they seek God? In God's providence the nurture of children is wisely left to parents. He uses us to prepare the hearts of our children to understand and to seek God.

One of the most familiar verses in the Bible reads, "Train up a child in the way he should go: and when he is old, he will not depart from it" (Proverbs 22:6). This is a command with a promise that has brought a great deal of comfort to the hearts of parents through the ages.

The thought of God looking down from heaven upon our children and upon us should inspire and motivate good training as we are obedient to His commands.

*. . . like [the child to which] a woman gives untimely birth, that has not seen the sun.* PSALM 58:8, AMPLIFIED

Deep disappointment and sadness comes when a premature birth takes place and the child does not live. The heart that has been anticipating joyfully the arrival of the infant is now heavy. Arms that have been longing for the soft littleness of a baby are now forlorn and empty. The Christian woman, should this happen to her, must rely on God's foreknowledge. "In God I have put my trust," must be our cry.

*I am become a stranger unto my brethren, and an alien unto my mother's children.* PSALM 69:8

David's complaint was born of distress that was real. You may be experiencing a relationship with loved ones that is not entirely satisfactory. Jesus' own brothers did not always believe in Him; we are told this in John's Gospel (7:5). David, too, encountered an alienation of family affection because of his loyalty to God.

63

Often a new baby in the family helps to soften and heal the wounds of misunderstanding among relatives. Our testimony must remain unshakable throughout all our family encounters.

*Upon Thee I have leaned from birth; it was Thou who took me from the maternal womb. My praise is continually of Thee. I have been a marvel to many, but Thou art my strong refuge. My mouth is filled with Thy praise and with Thy glory all day. Cast me not off in my old age; forsake me not now that my strength is spent. . . . O God, Thou hast taught me from my youth and I still declare Thy wonders. So even to old age and gray hairs, O God, do not forsake me, till I proclaim Thy might to this generation and Thy power to all descendants.*

PSALM 71:6–9, 17–18, BERKELEY

This prayer of an aged worshiper is a marvel of beauty. Reflecting on his life, David's heart is filled with praise. We have heard David speak before, declaring that it was God who took him from the maternal womb. It is a wonderful truth for the expectant mother to contemplate.

"Cast me not off in my old age" is a reminder for those of us whose parents are in the sunset years of life that there is a job for us to do. With tender, loving care our parents ministered to our every need when we were helpless and totally dependent upon them. How much we owe them! When their strength is spent, and old age and gray hairs have come to them, will we forsake them? God forbid!

I want to remember this Psalm, don't you? If old age comes to me, I shall want to proclaim God's might and power till my dying day. I shall also hope that my children will not forsake me.

*Had I spoken thus [and given expression to my feelings], I would have been untrue and have dealt treacherously against the generation of your children.* PSALM 73:15, AMPLIFIED

There are times in life, and the writer of this Psalm experienced it also, when we look at other people and wonder. We see the prosperity, the ease and manner in which many live. Especially do we wonder when we observe those outside of Christ who, from all outward appearances, are living an interesting, exciting, full life. They even blaspheme the name of God, and nothing seems to happen. We wonder, and we question.

Such were the thoughts of Asaph, who wrote this Psalm. If you read on you will discover him going into the sanctuary; as he meditates there, everything comes into focus. Men may succeed and be satisfied without God in this life. But, oh, consider the end of such people!

We need the far vision in our lives, don't we? For the sake of ourselves, our children, and our children's children, we need the spacious outlook that draws us close to God now, and keeps our gaze fixed on Him for future days and for eternity.

*My people, give ear to my instruction; listen to the words of my mouth, as I open my lips in a parable, as I utter lessons from ancient times, which we have heard and known, for our fathers related them to us. We do not conceal them from their children, recounting to the following generation the praises of the Lord and His might, yes, the wondrous works He has performed. . . . which He commanded our fathers to disclose to their sons, in order that the succeeding generation might know, that the children still to be born might arise and recount it to their sons, so as to put their confidence in God and not to forget God's works, but to keep His commandments.*

PSALM 78:1–7, BERKELEY

This is a reflective Psalm, skillfully showing the hand of God in history. Past failure is not minimized, but rather it is clearly shown, with the warning that events of the past are meant to teach. The godly Israelites taught these lessons to their children. The textbook was the Word which God had revealed. Their purpose was to bring up the children as worshipers of God, teaching them to adore Him and keep His laws. How did they

65

accomplish this? The method was a narration of the saving acts of God for His people. The school was the home, where the father took time and great pains to teach his children.

Your children, yet to be born, will learn these same truths if you are faithful in teaching them. The old, old story of God's redeeming love will be preserved from one generation to the other when parents recount the stories and instill a love for the Word in the hearts of their children.

*Yea, the sparrow hath found an house, and the swallow a nest for herself, where she may lay her young, even thine altars, O Lord of hosts, my King, and my God.* PSALM 84:3

Read the entire Psalm. This writer loved the Lord's house. Why, he almost envied the birds who could build their nests within the shadow of the altar, and who could place their young right there!

Today consider your attitude toward your church. How wonderful if we can say that we love the Lord's house with the same kind of devotion as this Psalmist!

*The Lord shall count, when he writeth up the people, that this man was born there. Selah.* PSALM 87:6

Do you know what *Selah* means? Well, it means "pause, and calmly think of that." So, right now, pause, and calmly think of what you have just read.

The Lord is keeping a written record. When I was a little girl, and when I was naughty, my little girlfriends would remind me that God was making a note of it in His big book. This idea was originated by a God-fearing grandmother whose sternness never left any doubts as to her knowledge. In later years, the love of God for His erring children became clear to me and my fear of the big black book with its awful record of my naughtiness was wiped away.

The fact stands—indisputably—that the Lord counts. He

it is who rejoices when He counts and writes that this man was born there. This speaks to the mature Christian of being born again.

Today read John 3.

*So teach us to number our days, that we may apply our hearts unto wisdom.* PSALM 90:12

Have you ever tried computing your life in days instead of years? Even being generous with the multiplication and use of figures, it results in a rather astonishing number of days—fewer than we like to think!

They tell us now that the threescore years and ten Moses speaks of in this Psalm are not to be considered an average life-span, that it was never intended as such to begin with, though it applied to the Israelites under the curse.

Days as such take on a new meaning during the pregnancy period. We learn to count backwards. That is, we say an average length of pregnancy is 280 days; so after it has been definitely established that we are "that way," we begin the countdown. They say that seventy percent of first births arrive after the scheduled date, but it is nice to count off the days hopefully! For most expectant women, the time seems to go fast, fast, fast—until usually the last month or two. Then, how eagerly we count off those days!

Perhaps we need to carry this idea on into the days after childbirth. Moses reminds us to number our days, and for good reason: ". . . that we may acquire discerning minds" (BERKE-LEY). (The old Hebrew word for "mind" is translated "heart.") Moses finishes his prayer, stating, ". . . let the beauty of the Lord our God be upon us . . ." (v. 17).

Would Christ's beauty show through each of us if we were more conscious of the actual brevity of life, and if we lived each day to its very fullest for Him?

*Know ye that the Lord he is God: it is he that hath made us, and not we ourselves [we are his]; we are his people, and the sheep of his pasture.* PSALM 100:3

This is a Psalm of thanksgiving. Maybe you are anticipating a Thanksgiving baby. We have had two arrive at that beautiful time of year.

A poet explained the marvel of God's creation:

### Baby

Where did you come from, baby dear?
  Out of the everywhere into here.
Where did you get those eyes so blue?
  Out of the sky as I came through.
What makes the light in them sparkle and spin?
  Some of the starry twinkle left in.
Where did you get that little tear?
  I found it waiting when I got here.
What makes your forehead so smooth and high?
  A soft hand stroked it as I went by.
What makes your cheek like a warm pink rose?
  I saw something better than anyone knows.
Whence that three-cornered smile of bliss?
  Three angels gave me at once a kiss.
Where did you get this pearly ear?
  God spoke, and it came out to hear.
Where did you get those arms and hands?
  Love made itself into bonds and bands.
Feet, whence did you come, you darling things?
  From the same box as the cherubs' wings.
How did they all just come to be you?
  God thought about me, and so I grew.
But how did you come to us, you dear?
  God thought about you, and so I am here.

GEORGE MACDONALD

*. . . a people yet to be born shall priase the Lord.*

PSALM 102:18, BERKELEY

We see the continuity of humanity set forth in these words from an afflicted soul. It is the birth process that has brought each of us into this world, and so it will always be. You had a mother, I had a mother; that is the way God planned it. The Word says, "The children of thy servants shall continue, and their seed shall be established before thee" (v. 28).

Abraham Lincoln said, "All that I am I owe to my mother," and so many others there are who can make the same claim. Unfortunately there are also many who can say it as a sad admission of many omissions on the part of a mother.

Mothers are often the recipients of the highest of tributes. To be worthy of such praise will call forth from you the greatest expenditure of time and effort ever required; it will never be equaled by anything else you may do in your lifetime. You will discover that a mother's devotion is not a matter of hours or days, but a full-time devotion.

Whether or not those yet to be born to you will praise the Lord must depend, in great measure, on your care and devotion as a mother.

*. . . as for the stork, the fir trees are her house.* PSALM 104:17

A book such as this just wouldn't seem quite complete if we didn't make mention of that famous bird associated with babies. Where the myth about storks bringing babies originated, I'm not quite certain, but the Bible certainly gives her no credit! "As for the stork, the fir trees are her house," and with that we trust we have helped set at nought the old wives' tale.

William Wordsworth eloquently reminds us:

> Our birth is but a sleep and a forgetting:
> The soul that rises with us, our life's star,
> Hath had elsewhere its setting,
> And cometh from afar:

Not in entire forgetfulness,
And not in utter nakedness,
But trailing clouds of glory do we come
From God, who is our home:
Heaven lies about us in our infancy!

"Intimations of Immortality"

The birth of a baby within a family where there are already
other children is a God-given opportunity to explain some of
the "facts of life" and to marvel at God's creative power. "God
gave us you, my dear; you came as a baby. And now, He is
going to give us another baby. . . ." Thus you can begin the
conversation with your other children. There are many helpful
books on the subject which will make explanations easier
for you. No longer need children wonder or parents worry
about how to tell. You will want to acquire such literature.

*Thy wife shall be as a fruitful vine by the sides of thine
house: thy children like olive plants round about thy table. . . .
Yea, thou shalt see thy children's children . . .*
PSALM 128:3, 6

The emblem for fruitfulness is traditionally a vine, just
as the olive plant signifies vigor, health, and a joyful life.
This is tender in meaning, even for those who are not ac-
customed to speaking their sentiments in quite this way. God's
blessings, we are shown, are attendant upon that home where
the family worships the Lord.

True strength within our families results when we are dili-
gent in our worship habits. True strength within our communities is evident, too, when our homes are God-centered.

*Surely I have behaved and quieted myself, as a child that
is weaned of his mother: my soul is even as a weaned child.*
PSALM 131:2

70

"The Lord didn't give women that equipment just for decoration!" It was the doctor speaking, the one who delivered our first two children. I was one of those know-it-all young mothers. I was not going to nurse my babies—that was old-fashioned. I was determined to be a "modern" mother by all the standards. What those standards were, I'm not at all certain. But I was wrong and I had to learn the hard way!

Our first born was a whopping, healthy eight-pounder who put in his squalling appearance at five o'clock in the afternoon of a miserably hot, Southern California September day. He thrived on formula and never had a sick day. The doctor and my good mother-in-law had urged me to nurse the child, but *I* knew better. And later, with a kind of smug satisfaction, I thought to myself, "Well, this child proves they were wrong!" So I thought!

Our second baby, a six-pound, ten-ounce girl, evaded being a Leap-Year baby by two hours. Tonia Ann's early months were worrisome. She could not keep the formula down and had more sick than healthy days. In our efforts to keep her alive, we tried all kinds of formula. Then, one day, my disheartened doctor said, "This child needed breast milk! The Lord didn't give women that equipment just for decoration!" As I went home from his office with my precious but sick baby daughter, I was a very concerned, deeply troubled, but far wiser young woman. Never have I blamed that doctor for saying what he did.

Since then we have had two more children, and I know what the Psalmist is speaking of when he referred to the cravings of the child being weaned.

*Thou didst possess my inward parts and didst weave me in my mother's womb. I praise Thee because I have been fearfully and wonderfully made; marvelous is Thy workmanship, as my soul is well aware. My bones were not hidden from Thee when I was made in secrecy and intricately fashioned*

71

*in utter seclusion. Thine eyes beheld my unformed substance, and in Thy book all was recorded and prepared day by day, when as yet none of them had being. How precious to me are Thy thoughts, O God!* PSALM 139:13–17, BERKELEY

The infinite knowledge of God is beyond human telling. Even the Psalmist, with his marvelous grasp of words and beautiful ability to give expression, finds himself limited, utterly without adequate means of explaining the all-seeing, all-knowing merciful God. We are lifted to lofty heights as we read this majestic Psalm. Our appreciation (a word grossly inadequate) of God penetrates our thinking as we read the innermost thoughts of David. Surely at such a time as this, your own heart echoes his words!

The woman in whose womb God is even now intricately fashioning and wonderfully making another body must thrill with even greater expectancy as she reads this magnificent description. Just think! It is God Himself who is performing this crowning achievement of creation within your very own body. Day by day, as the Psalmist describes, it is His control of your inward parts, and His weaving of life's material that will produce this child to whom you will give birth.

You will want to read this entire Psalm and praise God with an overflowing heart.

*My son, hear the instruction of thy father, and forsake not the law of thy mother.* PROVERBS 1:8

Solomon is to the Proverbs what David is to the Psalms. While Psalms was primarily a book of devotions, we see in Proverbs a practical guide to ethical living.

The Proverbs in the hands of loving parents can help them direct the conduct of their children. The intellectual attainments of Solomon were the wonder of his time; let us remember that we hold a key, as we read these words, to the wisdom of one learned in botany, zoology, politics, business, poetry, morality, and preaching. There are no scientific inaccuracies in the Proverbs. Napoleon is quoted as saying, "Nowhere is to be found such a series of beautiful ideas and admirable moral maxims, which pass before us like battalions of a celestial army. The soul never gets astray with this book for its guide."

*Be not wise in thine own eyes: fear the Lord, and depart from evil. It shall be health to thy navel, and marrow to thy bones.* PROVERBS 3:7, 8

The navel is the vital center of the body's well-being before birth. Marrow is the network of connective tissue, filled with blood vessels, within the bones. Solomon's comparison of true wisdom as the life lived completely in a right relationship to God is unexcelled when one considers the function of the navel.

Conception, fertilization; a new life has started. The developing embryo, which after three months can be called the fetus, is joined to the lining of the mother's uterus by means of the placenta which was formed before the embryo. Connecting the placenta with the fetus is the umbilical cord. Later, after birth, when the umbilical cord is cut, that little baby is on his own! The little depression in the middle of his abdomen is a life-long reminder that health and nourishment from the mother's blood were passed on to him through that cord. Your baby could not live if the placenta connecting the fetus by means of the umbilical cord did not function properly. How vital it is!

Perhaps at no other time in your life will the wisdom of Solomon be better understood by you than now as you consider all the depth and logic of his comparison. Ask your doctor to describe all the functions of the umbilical cord and the placenta. Perhaps he is familiar with this verse.

Mother-to-be, this is your noblest experience. Awed and flooded with tenderness, I know you must be. Pray now that the baby's tissues and organs will mature properly so that he will be ready for newborn existence. Reappraise your diet and other habits. Praise God for His wondrous provision for the precious new life resting safely within your body.

*The proverbs of Solomon. A wise son maketh a glad father: but a foolish son is the heaviness of his mother.* PROVERBS 10:1

One of the marvelous things about Solomon's proverbs is their self-conveying truth. Needing little or no explanation, these short statements are usually self-explanatory. One gets the feeling that he is reading something drawn from real experience.

The sharp contrasts drawn between wisdom and folly are so vividly set forth that one knows immediately that this is truth that abides. How much we and our children need to learn this truth and make it part of our daily experience! How much we shall need to remember and call forth this knowledge into practical application in the years ahead as we seek to instill virtues in the lives of our children.

*As a jewel of gold in a swine's snout, so is a fair woman which is without discretion.* PROVERBS 11:22

How discreet are you? Do you possess good judgment in your conduct and speech? It's a fair question and one that is directed toward self-examination. This proverb poses the question with its ludicrous comparison.

A news bulletin informs us that pigs are now setting the standards for feminine cosmetics. If pigs like 'em, women can use 'em with confidence!

In Beltsville, Maryland, the Food and Drug Administration has a new laboratory. Sure enough, out there the pigs are being served a blueplate of lipstick and hand lotion, with a side order of wrinkle remover. And guess what's for dessert? Mascara! That's right, you read correctly! If the two-hundred-pound pigs are pleased—and if their delicate skin doesn't turn scaly, if their livers don't go bad, and if their teeth don't fall out—you and I can relax with the assurance that we won't be poisoned.

But, you know, I haven't read of jewelry being tested by a pig. Can you picture a pig, just an ordinary pig, running around with a beautiful golden jewel in its snout? Ridiculous! The luster of the jewel would soon be destroyed by the dirty habits of the pig. The importance of discretion in our characters becomes evident as we see the contrast in Solomon's proverb.

God may have graciously endowed you with some degree of physical attractiveness, but beauty is not an advantage if you lack discretion. I know a husband who claims his wife was never more beautiful than when she was pregnant. There is a quality which shines forth in the happy, expectant mother which just breathes discretion.

*A wife with strength of character is a crown to her husband, but she who acts disgracefully is rottenness in his bones.*

PROVERBS 12:4, BERKELEY

The *I do's* we say at the marriage altar do not make good wives of us. There must follow real effort and willing submission, combined with a love that continues to give and grow, if our marriage is to be happy and blessed. This takes strength of character.

When husband and wife become parents, a new dimension of love develops. Then it is that a new depth in character is revealed as they yield themselves to the Lord, recognizing Him as the continuing Source of strength for all their needs. Two-plus-one equals more than three when the boundaries of married love are pushed back to include a new miracle of life.

*Every wise woman buildeth her house: but the foolish plucketh it down with her hands.* PROVERBS 14:1

Daniel Webster is credited with saying: "If we work upon

marble, it will perish; if we work upon brass, time will efface it; if we rear temples, they will crumble into dust; but if we work upon immortal minds, if we imbue them with principles, with the just fear of God and love of our fellow men, we engrave on those tablets something that will brighten to all eternity."

Yes, mothers are builders, sculptors of immortality, for the Bible tells us we are fellow workers for God (I Corinthians 3:9). How fortunate that woman who has asked God to be the Architect in her life, who is using His Word as her blueprint, and for whom Jesus Christ is the Foundation of her very existence. Such a woman is wise with the wisdom that comes from above. Her influence in the lives of her children will be of everlasting consequence.

### So Is a Mother's Influence

I took a piece of plastic clay
And idly fashioned it one day,
And as my fingers pressed it still,
It bent and yielded to my will.
I came again when day was past,
The bit of clay was hard at last.
The form I gave it still it bore,
But I could change that form no more.
I took a piece of living clay
And gently formed it day by day,
And molded it with power and art—
A young child's soft and yielding heart.
I came again when years were gone,
He was a man I looked upon.
The early imprint still he bore,
But I could change him then no more.

AUTHOR UNKNOWN

*He who spares his rod [of discipline] hates his son, but he who loves him diligently disciplines and punishes him early.*

PROVERBS 13:24, AMPLIFIED

The truth of this Scripture is repeated in the following verses (AMPLIFIED OLD TESTAMENT) which are quoted without additional comment: "Discipline your son while there is hope, but do not [indulge your angry resentments by undue chastisements and] set yourself to his ruin" (Proverbs 19:18); "Withhold not discipline from the child, for if you strike and punish him with the [reed-like] rod, he will not die. You shall whip him with the rod and deliver his life from Sheol [Hades, the place of the dead]" (Proverbs 23:13–14); "Foolishness is bound up in the heart of a child, but the rod of discipline will drive it far from him" (Proverbs 22:15); "The rod and reproof give wisdom, but a child left undisciplined brings his mother to shame" (Proverbs 29:15); "Correct your son, and he will give you rest; yes, he will give delight to your heart" (Proverbs 29:17).

*Children's children are the crown of old men; and the glory of children are their fathers.* PROVERBS 17:6

Someday, the Lord willing, you may be a grandparent! The years go swiftly from infancy to adulthood—far too swiftly! We soon discover that time is short, especially after our children come into the world.

T. DeWitt Talmadge, a widely-known preacher and lecturer of an older generation, had this to say on the subject:

"I wonder if all the heads of families realize that the opportunity of influencing their homes for Christ and heaven is very brief, and will soon be gone. For a while the house is full of voices and footsteps of children. Sometimes you feel that you can hardly stand the racket; it is a rushing this way and a rushing that way until Father and Mother are well-nigh beside themselves.

"But the years glide away. After a while the voices are not

so many and those that stay are more sedate. First this room becomes quiet and then that room. . . .

"Yes! Yes! The house, noisy now, will soon be still enough. Just as when you began housekeeping there were just the two of you, there will be just two again.

"Oh, the alarming brevity of infancy and childhood! The opportunity is glorious, but it soon passes. Parents may say at the close of life: 'What a pity we did not do more for the Christian training of our children while we had them with us!' But the lamentation will be of no avail. The opportunity had wings and vanished."

*Even a child is known by his doings, whether his work be pure, and whether it be right.* PROVERBS 20:11

Children are capable of almost anything, good and bad. As parents, we need to learn and believe this. We need to guard against being unapproachable about our youngsters' doings. Too often we are on the defensive, refusing to believe our child capable of any wrongdoing.

The Word tells us, "The heart is deceitful above all things, and desperately wicked" (Jeremiah 17:9). The verse that follows, however, gives reassurance: "I the Lord search the heart, I try the reins, even to give every man according to his ways, and according to the fruit of his doings" (v. 10).

It is always a happy experience to get out the children's "baby" books, to read of their sayings and doings, to look at their photographs. The recollections are precious memories which time can never destroy, though it may dim them somewhat. We smile, we frown, too; we may even shed a few tears. As we think about these children God has "loaned" to us, we become aware that each child is so different in his and her own way. Yet there is a pattern in each one that has been developing along similar lines.

In the record of each of my children's lives, the sweetest things I read tell of the development of their love for Jesus.

78

As the Amplified Old Testament puts it, "Even a child is known by his acts." Surely this gives cause for solemn reflection. How awesome and important motherhood is!

*As a bird that wandereth from her nest, so is a man that wandereth from his place.* PROVERBS 27:8

I couldn't begin to tell you how many baby birds we have nursed and tenderly cared for through the years. One of our daughters seems to have an affinity for these non-fledglings. We have never succeeded in keeping them alive longer than a day, however; in spite of the fact that we have stood over them patiently and lovingly, feeding them with an eye dropper, doing everything possible for them, they have always expired. Baby birds need the mother bird.

The writer of Proverbs may have had something like this in mind. Who can tell? Even as the mother bird invites disaster and courts danger when she flies too far from her nest of young, so it is with the mother (or father) who leaves her children too often (unnecessarily). A mother's place is in the home. Of course, there are occasions that warrant a mother leaving home, and no mother should be deprived of getting out and away from her duties every so often; but first and foremost home is where she is needed.

Make certain nothing or no one comes between you and the divinely appointed task to which God has called you.

*There is a generation that curseth their father, and doth not bless their mother . . .* PROVERBS 30:11

The Baseball-playing evangelist Billy Sunday scored many solid hits in his lifetime. To him we credit the following: "If you want to drive the devil out of the world, hit him with a cradle instead of a crutch"; "To train a boy in the way he should go, you must go that way yourself."

These statements are just another way of saying what the writer of Proverbs was attesting. In this chapter we are shown

79

four different kinds of generations (vv. 11–14), and there isn't a parent who would want their children to fall into any of these categories. The flamboyant Billy Sunday has thrown out to us something at which we should aim if we want our future generations to avoid the life Proverbs describes.

*Her children arise up, and call her blessed; her husband also, and he praiseth her.* PROVERBS 31:28

It is doubtful whether a more beautiful portrayal of the ideal wife and mother has ever been written. The footnotes of the *Amplified Old Testament* (page 411) have shed new light on this chapter, adding much to our understanding of its content:

"It is important to the purpose of this invaluable chapter that one realize that it is first of all intended for young men. No young man is prepared to mingle with girls and choose a wife until he has firmly grasped the wise and practical hints to be found here. And no girl is prepared to mingle with men and plan for marriage until she has mastered and acquired for herself the ideals of God's 'capable, intelligent and virtuous woman.' Obviously, as in this case, it is the mother's God-given task to provide youth with this information directly from its inspired source, letting them grow up with it in their consciousness."

If our children are to call us blessed, and our husbands are to praise us, it will come as a result of our devotion to God which, as this chapter clearly shows us, is to permeate every area and relationship of our lives.

Today carefully read and study this chapter, and II Peter 1:3–8, which lists the seven Christian virtues.

*To every thing there is a season, and a time to every purpose under the heaven: A time to be born, and a time to die . . .*
ECCLESIASTES 3:1–2

How important it is to recognize God's timing! Perhaps you are at the point where the days seem very long. And the nights! The days, and especially the sleepless, uncomfortable nights, toward the end of a pregnancy can seem interminable. At such moments the expectant mother may find herself envying the hamster for whom sixteen days is the duration of being with young.

Yes, to everything there is a season, a time to be born. For the mouse, this means about nineteen days; for the elephant, twenty-one months; for a rabbit, one month; for a horse, about eleven months, and so on. I suppose the moral to the story is to be thankful that even though you may feel like an elephant, you're not one!

This prayer-poem of a mother-to-be speaks of waiting patiently for God's timing:

### Prayer of a Mother-to-Be

A bit of life, astir, within me lies,
    Surging tremulously.
A miracle of God, for which I must
    Wait patiently.

And on the break of my excited sighs
    A tiny form
I've learned to know, to cherish, and to love—
    So near, so warm.

I cannot see, nor guess, his likeness yet,
    But I will love
The tiny features which he does possess
    As from above.

Such joy of self-fulfillment that I know:
    What pleasure rare!

Because a babe, a child, within me grows
    For me to bear.

Time passes fast, and soon this babe shall lie
    Upon my breast!
Oh! cherished thought to clasp this tiny one!
    What welcome guest!

Oh! how I secretly do pine for him—
    This bit of heaven—
Soon destined to be mine, a gift from God
    My Father given.

Dear Father, who forever rules on High
    And guides us all,
Who guards the very smallest birds of earth
    Lest they should fall.

Protect, I pray, my little one, while he
    Within me lies,
And fashion him in soul and spirit whole,
    To reach the skies.

Please make him sound of limb, of blemish free,
    For this I ask,
Of sturdy health and stalwart for his work
    To do his task.

This is my earnest, heartfelt hope for him—
    Please hear me pray—
Grant me a child in soul and body strong
    To lead Your way.

MAXINE LEE ROOSE

*If a man beget an hundred children, and live many years, so that the days of his years be many, and his soul be not filled with good . . . ; I say, that an untimely birth is better than he.*

ECCLESIASTES 6:3

Solomon, the writer of Ecclesiastes, was striving to show that life is futile and not worth living if the soul is not right. But all we can say is, "Thank you." Yes, thanks to the Holy Spirit who, through the writer, has indeed shown us that life lived apart from God is a tragic waste.

This becomes doubly important as we, appreciating each today, anticipating each tomorrow, become keenly aware that our souls must be filled with good if our influence upon our children is to be of Christ-likeness.

*Therefore the Lord himself shall give you a sign; Behold, a virgin shall conceive, and bear a son, and shall call his name Immanuel.* ISAIAH 7:14

This is a Messianic prophecy. How thrilling it is to compare Scripture verses and to see the Old fulfilled in the New! Today read Matthew 1:23 and Luke 1:31, and marvel anew at God's redemptive plan.

Martha Snell Nicholson, beloved poet, has expressed this so poignantly in her poem "Suppose":

> Suppose that Christ had not been born
> That far away Judean morn.
> Suppose that God, Whose mighty hand
> Created worlds, had never planned
> A way for man to be redeemed.
> Suppose the wise men only dreamed
> That guiding star whose light still glows
> Down through the centuries. Suppose
> Christ never walked here in men's sight,
> Our blessed Way, and Truth, and Light.
> Suppose He counted all the cost,

And never cared that we were lost,
And never died for you and me,
    Nor shed His blood on Calvary
Upon the shameful cross. Suppose
    That having died, He never rose,
And there was none with power to save
    Our souls from death beyond the grave!
O far away Judean morn,
    Suppose that Christ had not been born!

*Behold, I and the children whom the Lord hath given me
are for signs and for wonders in Israel* ... ISAIAH 8:18
Yes, Isaiah was a father. Isaiah's name and the names of
the two children whom the Lord gave to him were actually
"signs" suggestive of the coming crisis and the need of God's
help for the Israelites.

What kind of a father do you suppose Isaiah was? I think
Isaiah spent time with his children, don't you? Fathers need
to get to know their children. Both suffer, the children and the
father, when they do not really get to know each other
through satisfying experiences.

### Two Prayers

Last night my little boy
Confessed to me
Some childish wrong;
And, kneeling at my knee,
He prayed with tears—
"Dear God, make me a man
Like Daddy—wise and strong;
I know You can."

Then while he slept
I knelt beside his bed,

Confessed my sins,
And prayed with low-bowed head,
"Oh, God, make me a child
Like my child here—
Pure, guileless,
Trusting Thee with faith sincere."

ANDREW GILLIES

*For unto us a child is born, unto us a son is given . . .*
ISAIAH 9:6

The first seven verses of this chapter are considered one of the greatest Messianic passages in the Old Testament. Read them carefully; then turn to Luke 1:32–33 and Luke 2:11 to find their fulfillment.

At such a time in your own experience, doesn't the fact of the Saviour's prophesied coming stir your heart? Dwell on the glorious fact that He came as a Child, and that the same Lord of hosts who performed this miracle (Isaiah 9:7), will perform the miracle of birth in your life.

*And there shall come forth a rod out of the stem of Jesse, and a Branch shall grow out of his roots.* ISAIAH 11:1

When the Apostle Paul stood up in the synagogue at Antioch and preached his great sermon, he recited some of the history of the Jewish nation. Included in his discourse was a reference to this very verse in Isaiah, "I have found David the son of Jesse, a man after mine own heart, which shall fulfil all my will. Of this man's seed hath God according to his promise raised unto Israel a Saviour, Jesus" (Acts 13:22–23).

We may find ourselves repeating a little verse by George MacDonald, which follows.

They were all looking for a king
To slay their foes and lift them high;
Thou cam'st, a little baby thing
That made a woman cry.

*He shall feed his flock like a shepherd: he shall gather the lambs with his arm, and carry them in his bosom, and shall gently lead those that are with young.* ISAIAH 40:11

An artist's beautiful portrayal of Jesus as the Good Shepherd, gently carrying a little lamb in His arms, is dearly loved by children and adults. The inspiration for this well-known painting came from this passage and others which bear similar reference (see Hebrews 13:20; I Peter 2:25; 5:4). The appeal of the painting is so universal because in it we see the Fatherhood of God, and the gentle tenderness of Love personified. No wonder both adults and children are attracted to it.

Before giving birth to her fourth baby, a dear friend wrote: "I always feel so much closer to God when I am expecting, because truly, this is such a wonderful gift from him. I must say, when I look at my three little ones, and feel the fourth one moving within me, '. . . my cup runneth over [Psalm 23:5].' "

Today read the Shepherd's Psalm and draw close to Him who gently leads those who are with young.

*Thus saith the Lord, thy redeemer, and he that formed thee from the womb, I am the Lord that maketh all things; that stretcheth forth the heavens alone; that spreadeth abroad the earth by myself.* ISAIAH 44:24

Creator and Redeemer—yes, He is both.

Mothers, too, have been called "creators second only to God." Yes, they are molders and makers of men; but God is still the Giver and Sustainer of life.

It was Charles Dickens who said, "I love little people; and

86

it is not a slight thing when they, who are so fresh from God, love us."

*Can a woman forget her sucking child, that she should not have compassion on the son of her womb? yea, they may forget, yet will I not forget thee.*  ISAIAH 49:15

It seems impossible that a mother would ever forget her children, yet the Word says this may happen. The comparison is made to show that God, however, will never forget His own.

*As one whom his mother comforteth, so will I comfort you . . .*  ISAIAH 66:13

The preceding verses (from v. 7 on) use the illustration of travail and childbirth to prophesy that Israel one day will become a recognized nation again. In our day we have seen this come to pass.

Is this to be your first child? Do not let the thought of travail and pain frighten you. It is an inexplainably sweet and blessed sort of labor. Think ahead to what it will bring forth. The effort and pain are quickly forgotten in the great joy that overwhelms you as you hear that longed-for first cry of your new-born child. In the days following, as you look at the helplessness of your child, realizing how much he needs and depends on you, this verse will come to mind. Somehow, as you go about caring for and comforting your little one, it will speak assurance to you. You will know that you can call upon Him to renew your strength, to supply your needs and those of your child.

*The word of the Lord came to me, Before I fashioned you in the womb I knew you, and before you were born I dedicated you; I designated you for a prophet to the nations.*
JEREMIAH 1:4–5, BERKELEY

The same Lord Who fashioned the Prophet Jeremiah, dedicating and designating him as a great prophet even before he was born, is in control of your life and that of your unborn child. These are staggering thoughts, profound in implication and hidden meaning. Praise Him for His greatness!

*. . . which their fathers taught them.* JEREMIAH 9:14

Preceding chapters have revealed the deep anguish of the prophet's heart over the sins of the people. Much of their sinfulness was the result of things their fathers had taught them. How plain the Word is in laying before parents the need for right teaching!

George Herbert, beloved English poet, wrote, "One good mother is worth a thousand schoolmasters." Education is a valuable asset in life, but parents—mothers, in particular—imbue a child with character, that highly important something our schools cannot give!

A person's education may be a great social and commercial asset in his lifetime; but the true measure of a man's worth is going to be found in the state of his soul. It is what we, as parents, teach our children, rather than their scholastic attainments, that will determine their greatest worth.

Will it someday be said of you, "Their parents taught them well"?

*Thy words were found, and I did eat them; and thy word was unto me the joy and rejoicing of mine heart . . .*
JEREMIAH 15:16

The Prophets Jeremiah and Ezekiel, and the beloved Disciple John, said the same thing. (See Ezekiel 3 and Revelation 10:9–10).

If joy and rejoicing, a sweetness like honey, followed the "eating" of the Word for these men, surely a diet of the Word for us is a necessity today!

The expectant mother is frequently admonished by her doctor to include certain essentials in her diet and to eliminate those foods that will not contribute to good health for herself and the child she is carrying. Allow the testimony of Jeremiah, Ezekiel, and John to influence your diet! Joy and rejoicing are promised—sweetness, too!

*Thus saith the Lord; A voice was heard in Ramah, lamentation, and bitter weeping; Rachel weeping for her children refused to be comforted for her children, because they were not.* JEREMIAH 31:15

Motherhood brings its share of joys and sorrows. There is laughter, great joy, and much happiness; but there are also tears, sorrow, and weeping. We must prepare our hearts for both.

This particular lamentation is a forecast of the bitter experience the mothers of the slaughtered babes of Bethlehem would endure many centuries later. The actual fulfillment of this can be seen in Matthew 2:17 "Then was fulfilled that which was spoken by Jeremy the prophet. . . ."

In an attempt to kill the Christ-Child, the wicked King Herod ordered the death of all Hebrew children two years old and younger. Can you imagine the bitter weeping? Our mother-hearts today, after so many years on this side of the cross, are deeply touched. When our hearts are pained with the cares and burdens of parenthood, let us remember those who have preceded us, who, like us, were parents with emotions just as real as ours.

*Observe! All souls are Mine; the soul of the father as well as the soul of the son is Mine; it is the person that sins who shall die.* EZEKIEL 18:4, BERKELEY

The Bible tells us that "The fathers have eaten sour grapes, and the children's teeth are blunted" (Jeremiah 31, 29, BERKELEY). It means that people were blaming their unhappy condition, whatever it might have been, on their fathers. Especially they maintained this attitude of injured innocence when they were suffering, declaring, in effect, that they were bearing the punishment for sins they had not committed.

It was a rather astonishing thing, therefore, to have the Prophet Ezekiel come along and tell them that wickedness was not hereditary! We can well imagine the Prophet's unpopularity at this point. "As I live, says the Lord God, you shall not have occasion any more to use this proverb in Israel" (v. 3, AMPLIFIED).

Today read Romans 6:23 for New Testament verification of this verse.

*The king then ordered Ashpenaz, chief of his eunuchs, to bring in for service in his palace some Israelites of the royal family and of the nobility—boys without any defects, good-looking, versed in various studies, well informed, with intelligent views, fit to take their place in the royal palace . . .*

DANIEL 1:3–4, BERKELEY

This reads like a "What's What" with the "Who's Who" of Nebuchadnezzar's day—or any day, for that matter! Most parents would agree that these qualifications would be difficult to improve upon at any time!

The story of Daniel and his three friends is perhaps one of the better-known Bible stories. The strength of character that Daniel in particular manifested is a beautiful story. We see in Daniel and his companions ideal young manhood. They did not acquire their loyalty to the faith of their fathers, however, overnight.

We do not know about the parents of these brave young lads; but whoever they were, they had done a good job of training their sons. They knew God!

The most important aspect of our responsibility as fathers and mothers is that which involves early training of our children so that they may know God, love His Word, and accept His Son as Saviour.

*I thank thee, and praise thee, O thou God of my fathers . . .*

This is the conclusion of a beautiful prayer of blessing Daniel uttered after he and his companions had sought God's mercy concerning interpretation of the king's troubled dream.

Daniel acknowledged that it was God who had given him wisdom and might. He was aware of the power available to him through prayer. His was no "emergency brake" appeal applied in a moment of desperate need, but a natural turning to the Lord from an intimate relationship nurtured through the years.

One of the most appealing and reassuring things a child can do is to acknowledge in a time of personal or family need the fact that he has the Lord to whom he can turn. Such a statement can issue only from the lips of that child who knows Jesus in a personal way. Such a child, like Daniel, could say, "O thou God of my fathers. . . ."

*Tell ye your children of it, and let your children tell their children, and their children another generation.* JOEL 1:3

The messages of four prophets—Hosea, Joel, Amos, and Obadiah—which are carried in the books of the Bible bearing their names, are demonstrative of the apostasy of their time. The charges laid against the people describe the moral and spiritual degradation into which they had fallen.

Acquaint yourself with the messages of the Minor Prophets, so that you can tell your children of them. It has been said that tomorrow's world will be a healthier one with Bible-based, God-fearing men and women who became that way in their earlier years.

*And should not I spare Nineveh, that great city, wherein are more than sixscore thousand persons that cannot discern between their right hand and their left hand . . . ?*

JONAH 4:11

91

God has concern for non-discerners! Those words could summarize this chapter, for God's compassion for little children is clearly set forth in His concern for 120,000 of them in one city. Jonah had prophesied that judgment and doom would fall upon Nineveh for its great wickedness. When the people of the city believed God and repented, God revoked the sentence of evil, and the city and its inhabitants, including the precious children, were saved.

Instead of Jonah feeling gladness, we see him resentful and displeased. He complained bitterly to God. He did not appreciate God's mercy! Jonah thought more of his reputation as a prophet, than of the lives of 120,000 children and the others in the great city.

How we need to thank God for His great fatherly love which showed itself on behalf of Nineveh's children. It is available for our children, as well.

*But thou, Bethlehem Ephratah, though thou be little among the thousands of Judah, yet out of thee shall he come forth unto me that is to be ruler in Israel; whose goings forth have been from of old, from everlasting.* MICAH 5:2

Is your imagination working? Can you picture this scene?

Long, long years ago, a Prophet stood under the starry sky, raised his eyes heavenward, and prayed, "O God, is there hope? Is there any hope for this sinful, rebellious people?"

Listen! Can you hear the voice of God as He answered the distressed Prophet? "Yes, Micah, there is hope."

The prophet is crying again, "But when, and where?"

The answer comes in the words of our Scripture meditation, ". . . in Bethlehem. . . ."

This time the Prophet is perplexed, even doubtful. "Bethlehem . . . Bethlehem. But it's one of the smaller tribes!"

The voice of God came again. We can read the fulfillment of this prophecy in our New Testament Gospel accounts, and every December 25 the world celebrates Christmas and Christians remember Christ's birthday. The destiny of this Babe affected all mankind.

*And the streets of the city shall be full of boys and girls playing in the streets thereof.* ZECHARIAH 8:5

The Prophet Zechariah is drawing a picture, as it were, of a prosperous and peaceful Zion, the restoration of Jerusalem. To the eye of a watchful parent, it is indeed a picture of peace and serenity when children can safely play in the streets. The prophetic promise is one of perfect safety and freedom.

Frequently one reads in his paper or hears on the radio a tragic story of a child whose life has been taken because he ran out into the street and was struck by a car. It is a danger that hangs over the head of every boy and girl. The parents' role in teaching and warning children of such a danger is a very vital part of the growing-up and learning process.

When we have done our best to teach them well, we must be ever watchful in those tender, just-learning years, and surround our children with our prayers petitioning God for His guardianship.

*Now the birth of Jesus Christ was on this wise: When as his mother Mary was espoused to Joseph, before they came together, she was found with child of the Holy Ghost.*
MATTHEW 1:18

Without question, the birth of Jesus Christ was the greatest occurrence since the creation of the world. This divine event was the goal of all Old Testament prophecy; it was the crisis point of history. And it is stated so simply, with such appealing restraint. Did ever a King have such an obscure birth before or since?

It is difficult to try to imagine how frightened and overcome with awe the little virgin of Nazareth must have been at the announcement that she was to give birth to a Child through the power of the Holy Spirit. It is equallly difficult to put one's self in the place of Joseph and try to understand his reaction.

Today, as you think about the earthly parents of our Lord, let the greatness of their characters, their devotion, their faith in God and love and trust for each other, even in the face of slander, gossip and misunderstanding, serve as an inspiration to you and your husband. Read and compare the narratives of this wondrous event in Matthew and Luke.

*Now when Jesus was born in Bethlehem of Judaea in the days of Herod the king, behold, there came wise men from the east to Jerusalem, Saying, Where is he that is born King of the Jews? for we have seen his star in the east, and are come to worship him.* MATTHEW 2:1–2

A journey of many months was involved in the visit of these Wise Men. Such important visitors! Little did they realize the importance of their trip, for it is almost certain that their gifts enabled the poor parents of the Child to flee to Egypt, escaping the jealous Herod's slaughter of Hebrew children.

The arrival of the Wise Men with their retinue must surely have aroused the curiosity of the entire city of Jerusalem and the surrounding countryside. The very thought of a potential rival to his throne sent the wicked Herod into a mad frenzy. Herod was the man who missed Christmas. How many there are like him in the world today!

*And when they were come into the house, they saw the young child with Mary his mother, and fell down, and worshipped him: and when they had opened their treasures, they presented unto him gifts; gold, and frankincense, and myrrh.* MATTHEW 2:11

Your child will no doubt be the recipient of gifts. I am sure the gratitude of Joseph and Mary knew no bounds, nor could they adequately express the thankfulness that welled up within them. You will experience deep gratitude, too, when the visitors and gifts, the tokens from loving hearts, arrive. Let your thankfulness overflow, inadequate as it may seem.

The Wise Men returned to their own country by another way, having been warned in a dream not to return to Herod. Have you ever thought about that? It has been suggested that they would have gone another way even without the dream, for all truly wise men go another way after they have found the Christ. Perhaps because of your Christ-honoring attitude, there will be those who will leave much wiser for having visited your child.

*. . . the disciples came to Jesus with the question, "Who is really greatest in the Kingdom of Heaven?" Jesus called a little child to His side and set him on his feet in the middle of them all. "Believe me," he said, "unless you change your whole outlook and become like little children you will never enter the Kingdom of Heaven. It is the man who can be as humble as this little child who is 'greatest' in the Kingdom of Heaven.*

*"Anyone who welcomes one child like this for My sake is welcoming me. But if anyone leads astray one of these little children who believe in me he would be better off thrown into the depths of the sea with a millstone hung round his neck! Alas for the world with its pitfalls! In the nature of things there must be pitfalls, yet alas for the man who is responsible for them!"* MATTHEW 18:1–7, PHILLIPS

Jesus called a precious little child to His side, and in that tender act showed His disciples (and us) what it really means to be humble. Can you picture Him? Jesus, so full of compassion, yet so manly, places His hands around the waist of the child, lifting this personification of innocence into the disciples' midst. As He puts the child down gently, He looks with loving-kindness into the bewildered faces of the disciples and gives them a beautiful lesson in true humility! A harmless little child was used by the Master Teacher to teach all of us one of the most important lessons to be learned if we would be His followers.

One of the greatest joys of having children comes as we allow ourselves to be taught by them! This may seem to be a paradox, but it was Christ Himself who showed us its implications.

*"Be careful that you never despise a single one of these little ones—for I tell you that they have angels who see My Father's face continually in Heaven."*

MATTHEW 18:10, PHILLIPS

Here Jesus is teaching angelic protection, especially for children. It is a teaching that speaks reassurance to the heart of a mother.

Elsewhere the Word tells us, "The angel of the Lord encampeth round about them that fear him . . ." (Psalm 34:7).

*Then were there brought unto him little children, that he should put his hands on them, and pray: and the disciples rebuked them. But Jesus said, Suffer little children, and forbid them not, to come unto me: for of such is the kingdom of heaven. And he laid his hands on them, and departed thence.*

MATTHEW 19:13-15

Again we see Jesus showing His interest in little children. Christ was very interested in families. (Read the same account in Luke 18:15–18, and Mark 10:13–16.)

What is it about the child that is so appealing? What was Jesus referring to when He said that heaven will be occupied by childlike people? Is it not their lovableness? Children are so free of pretense, of pride. How teachable they are! How trusting!

Jesus became indignant when the disciples tried to keep the children away, thinking the Master should not be bothered by them. How wrong they were, they quickly learned, as He lovingly extended His arms to the little ones.

This is a picture which every mother holds close in her thoughts; it makes the expectant woman's heart leap with anticipatory joy.

*. . . woe unto that man by whom the Son of man is betrayed! it had been good for that man if he had not been born.*
MATTHEW 26:24

Judas! Yes, what of this one? Jesus said it would have been better if he had not even been born!

Have you ever thought about Judas' mother? Where was she when her son betrayed our Lord? What kind of a person was she? Her pain must surely have crushed her. The following poem speaks eloquently of what might have happened:

## Two Mothers

Long, long ago, so old legends relate,
Two mothers once met at an old city gate.
"By the look in your eyes," said the one to the other,
"I see that you, too, must have once been a mother."
"And by the blue-tinted veil on your hair,
You, too, have know sorrow and deepest despair."
"Ah, yes," she replied, "I once had a son,
A sweet little lad, full of laughter and fun.
But tell of your child."—"Oh, I knew he was blest
From the moment I first held him close to my breast.
And my heart almost burst with the joy of that day."
"Ah, yes," said the other, "I felt the same way."
The former continued. "The first steps he took,
So eager and breathless—the sweet startled look
Which came over his face. He trusted me so—"
"Ah, yes," said the other, "I felt the same glow."

97

"How often I shielded and spared him from pain,
And when he for others was so cruelly slain,
When they crucified him—and they spat in his face,
How gladly I would have hung in his place!"
A moment of silence—"Oh, then you are she,
The mother of Christ," and she fell on one knee;
But the blessed one raised her up, drawing her near,
And kissed from the cheek of the woman a tear.
"Tell me the name of the son you loved so,
That I may share with you your grief and your woe."
She lifted her eyes, looking straight at the other:
"He was Judas Iscariot. I am his mother."

RICHARD MAXWELL

*He saith unto them, How many loaves have ye? go and see. And when they knew, they say, Five, and two fishes.*

MARK 6:38

Great crowds of people followed Jesus and the disciples wherever they went. On this particular occasion they were in a desert place, far removed from any villages, and the people were hungry.

The Word tells us that when Jesus saw the multitudes of people He was moved with compassion toward them. His heart went out then, as it does now. A friend has put into poetic form a beautiful sentiment that embraces this scene:

A Mother's Gift

Lord, my offering isn't much,
I give myself to Thee—
My heart, my hands, my thoughts, my time,
In deep humility.

I know that You can take these gifts
And by Your special touch—
Transform, refine, magnify,
Turning little into much.

I remember, Lord, how You took the loaves
And the fish beside the sea,
And broke them among the multitude
That had come to learn of Thee.

If You can feed a multitude—
The thousands that were there,
With five loaves of bread and two small fish
With twelve basketsfull to spare,

What can You do with a Mother's heart,
Her thoughts, her work, her day,
When they are given to Thee, Lord,
To be used in Thine own way?

NAOMI LANCE

*Therefore I say unto you, What things soever ye desire,
when ye pray, believe that ye receive them, and ye shall
have them.* MARK 11:24

The director of a Christian home for unwanted and under-
privileged children has made the statement that everything he
has learned about prayer has come largely from the lips of
these boys and girls.

Parents who take the time to pray with their children, and
listen to the prayers of their children, will agree. The simple
reality voiced by the praying child is touching beyond comparison.

This same director told of a little boy who prayed, "Lord,
it's a strange world we are living in. Cars have engines. Engines

need gas and oil to make them run. You know Lord, even dogs have their problems—the mothers get pregnant! Well, that's just the way it is, Lord . . ."

Yes, that's the way it is, Lord. The dear little child says just what's in his heart; there is no hypocrisy. Oh, may we ever be teachable! And more simple! May we be alert, too, to what the Word and Jesus Himself has to say about prayer.

*But the angel said unto him, Fear not, Zacharias: for thy prayer is heard; and thy wife Elisabeth shall bear thee a son, and thou shalt call his name John.* LUKE 1:13

Dear old faithful Zacharias, busily performing his priestly duties in the Temple, was suddenly filled with fear as an angel of the Lord appeared to him. But if the angel's presence surprised him, Zacharias was even more troubled and afraid after hearing the angel's message. It is not difficult to imagine his astonishment. "How can this be? Why—I'm an old man, and my wife is beyond the childbearing years . . ."

The angel's answer reassured the elderly man: "I am Gabriel, that stand in the presence of God; and am sent to speak unto thee, and to shew thee these glad tidings" (v. 19). If Zacharias had been anything other than the godly man he was, he might not have accepted this. Corruption among the priests in the Temple was a known fact. But from that moment on, and until the child was born, Zacharias remained speechless, as the angel had said he would.

In spite of his inability to speak to Elisabeth, Zacharias did communicate the angel's message to his wife. Together they must have rejoiced as they eagerly awaited the birth of the son of whom the angel had said, ". . . he shall be great in the sight of the Lord, . . . and he shall be filled with the Holy Ghost, even from his mother's womb. And many of the children of Israel shall he turn to the Lord their God." (vv. 15-16).

100

*And thou shalt have joy and gladness; and many shall rejoice at his birth.* LUKE 1:14

Such a beautiful promise for a father and mother-to-be! What wonderful words to cling to through nine months of waiting—which at times can seem much longer! How truly blessed Zacharias and Elisabeth were!

Elisabeth was a humble soul. She did not mount a spiritual pedestal when she learned that she was going to be the mother of a baby who would be filled with the Holy Spirit. As a mother whose influence in shaping her son's life was to be so important, she exhibited a Spirit-filled self that God could bless and use.

The birth of a child does bring great joy and gladness. And many there are—friends, relatives—who do rejoice with us. Pray that the joy may be long-lasting, that this child will develop in your home under your parental guidance and influence to bring joy and gladness as his life shows forth his love for Jesus.

*Fear not, Mary: for thou hast found favour with God.*
LUKE 1:30

Lovely, sweet, young, favored girl—that was Mary. Favored? Yes, but deservedly. Pure? Assuredly. Wholly consecrated? Motives altogether clear. Devoted? With all her heart. Loving? God first—deeply, trustfully—others next, self last.

But was she fearful? Momentarily. Why? Wouldn't you have been? Consider the facts. She was young, very young. She'd never been visited by an angel, and the angel's announcement was enough to put fear into the most devout heart. And Mary wasn't married yet. The angel's explanation that it was God who was going to bring all of this about quieted the pounding of her heart, and she could relax, confident that everything would be alright.

And you can relax, too. Committed to Him, obedient to His message to you, you and your unborn child are assured of His favor. Whatever happens to you, it is His will, and you can respond as Mary did: "Behold the handmaid of the Lord; be it unto me according to thy word" (v. 38).

*... when Elisabeth heard the salutation of Mary, the babe leaped in her womb ...* LUKE 1:41

Of course, Mary wanted to be with her cousin Elisabeth when she heard (from the angel) that Elisabeth was expecting a son also. She went with haste (v. 39). No doubt she just couldn't get there fast enough. How wonderful! To think that Elisabeth, old as she was, was going to have a baby! Mary wanted to be with her during the last three months of her pregnancy. She wanted to confide in her cousin. She wanted to help her.

Did Elisabeth know about Mary? No, no, she did not. But the moment Mary spoke, the baby leaped within Elisabeth for joy. Together they shared the joy that filled their hearts to overflowing. Together they praised and thanked God that He should count them worthy.

If you have a friend, or know someone who is in the same condition as you are now, this would be a wonderful moment for you to call her. Ask her to read about Elisabeth and Mary.

*Now Elisabeth's full time came that she should be delivered; and she brought forth a son. And her neighbours and her cousins heard how the Lord had shewed great mercy upon her; and they rejoiced with her.* LUKE 1:57-58

The circumstances surrounding the birth of Elisabeth's son were far different from those you will experience. Our immaculate hospital conditions in no way compare with the simple, primitive surroundings in which John was to enter the world. The crisp efficiency of attending nurses will be welcomed by you and will give you much confidence as you lie in waiting. But consider how it must have been for Elisabeth. And then, she brought forth her son!

But here the differences between Elisabeth and you end. They really do! Good news travels fast, especially when it concerns the safe arrival of a new baby. Your dear husband just won't be able to get to that phone booth fast enough! And how he will fumble for coins, for that list of names and telephone numbers you so carefully made out for him! It's funny, yet wonderful! The neighbors and relatives are anxious to know, and the proud new father is anxious to tell.

But Elisabeth's husband couldn't talk; and he didn't have a phone handy. Notwithstanding these problems, the neighbors and kinfolk (v. 58) heard the good news. But what did they hear? How the Lord had shown great mercy upon Elisabeth! I can just imagine Elisabeth herself saying to the midwife who had helped deliver the child, "Tell my cousins and neighbors how the Lord has shown great mercy upon me. . . . Tell them we have a beautiful baby boy, a son at last. . . ."

Yes, Elisabeth was old, well advanced in years, past the normal childbearing age, and her first reaction would surely have been one of deep gratitude for God's great mercy.

*Whatever will this little boy be then? For the hand of the Lord was so evidently with him—protecting and aiding him.*
LUKE 1:66, AMPLIFIED

The Jewish custom of circumcising the infant on the eighth day was being observed. Zacharias and Elisabeth were about to have this ancient rite performed on their child, at which time they would name the baby. Quite naturally everyone assumed that the only son of this couple would be called Zacharias, after his father. However, it was Elisabeth who stepped in and said, "Not so; but he shall be called John" (v. 60). Turning to the father and using signs, the people inquired what he would have the child called. Zacharias asked for a writing tablet and wrote, "His name is John" (v. 63).

The astonishment of the people was great. They were even more awed when Zacharias opened his mouth and began to speak. Remember, this man hadn't uttered a word for nine months!

Zacharias' first words were praise, blessing, and thankfulness to God for what He had done. How wonderful!

Just imagine the reaction of the people! The word spread like wildfire throughout the hill country of Judea. The reaction was the same everywhere: Whatever will this little boy be? The hand of the Lord was so evident upon him and his parents.

Today read the rest of this first chapter of Luke (vv. 67-80). Picture the fatherly love of old Zacharias as he tenderly looked at his dear son and said, "And you, little one, shall be called prophet of the Most High. . . ."

*And all went to be taxed, every one into his own city. And Joseph also went up from Galilee, out of the city of Nazareth, into Judaea, unto the city of David, which is called Bethlehem; . . . To be taxed with Mary his espoused wife, being great with child.* LUKE 2:3-5

What a long, weary journey—about ninety miles, it is estimated—for a woman expecting a baby! How would you like to make a trip like that on the not-so-soft back of a donkey right about now? Women in "your condition" just aren't supposed to be doing things like that, you would say.

Slowly, Mary and Joseph plod along in answer to the Roman Emperor's edict. The sweet, gentle young woman on the back of the patient donkey is talking: "Joseph, Joseph, you are so kind, so good to me, but don't feel badly about this trip. Remember, the prophets have foretold that in the town of David the Messiah would be born. God is sending us to Bethlehem. It will be all right. . . ."

And those two, who knew the old Jewish Scriptures so well, must have taken great comfort and encouragement as they made that long, hard journey, remembering and sharing with each other the words of prophecy.

104

When your husband speeds you to the hospital for you to give birth to your child, remember the journey another couple made almost two thousand years ago. The contrast is great, but there is a common bond—a child is about to be born. And Mary, if she could reach out and give you a word of encouragement, would surely say, "It's a wonderful experience. I'm so happy for you! Don't be fearful. My Son and our heavenly Father will love and help you. You are not alone in this greatest of all womanly experiences."

*And so it was, that, while they were there, the days were accomplished that she should be delivered.* LUKE 2:6

Mary was about to become a mother! And so are you!! The time for her delivery had come. Yours is approaching.

How exciting it is to feel the soft new "little things" your infant son or daughter will soon be wearing! Perhaps you have been pleasantly surprised by a baby shower. Everything is in readiness. The bassinette—borrowed or new, pink or blue, it won't matter when that tiny one is brought to you—the little undershirt, the diaper, the sweetest nightgown, and the receiving blanket—all packed and waiting to enfold this little bit of love sent from heaven above.

Consider again, will you, what it was like for Mary when her days completed and birth was due. The Word tells us, "And she brought forth her firstborn son, and wrapped him in swaddling clothes . . ." (v. 7).

I shall never forget what happened in our home one Christmas. One of our little girls came and asked me for "a nice white rag for the Baby Jesus." As I followed her back to her play, I couldn't help but wonder what was going on. "See, Mommy, the doll is going to be the Baby Jesus, and He didn't wear a pink dress." She shook her head with emphasis and proceeded to wrap the doll in the "nice white rag."

Big brother, with twelve-year-old wisdom, provided the explanation. "It's like this, Mom. I told her I was pretty certain the Baby Jesus didn't have a nice little dress when He was born. I know the Bible says 'swaddling clothes.' I figured maybe it was something like those white rags you use for washing windows."

A rag is a rag, and there's really nothing nice about it. It may be clean, soft, and white, but it's still just a rag. The youngsters didn't mean any harm, but, unknown to them, they were depicting an unfortunate truth that began with the Christ-Child's birth, characterized His earthly life, and has lasted through succeeding generations. Too many still give Him the rag's end of time, money, interest and love!

How can *you* show your love for Christ this day?

*. . . because there was no room or place for them in the inn.* LUKE 2:7, AMPLIFIED

In his book *My Favorite Christmas Story* Roy Rogers has described the inn scene of that night in a way that touched my heart deeply. Roy says, "The courtyard of the inn was jammed with donkeys and camels and swearing, weary men. The inn was crowded; there wasn't even standing room. Joseph must have known there wouldn't be any room for him and his Mary, but he knocked anyway. What else could he do?

Knock, knock, knock. A baby is about to be born. The most important baby ever to be born on this earth. Let us in, let Him in, out of the cold and the night. Knock, knock, knock.

The sleepy innkeeper came rubbing his eyes, and opened the door. He didn't waste any words; he just told them there wasn't any room. They'd have to go somewhere else.

"No room." They are the most heart-rending words in the Bible. No room. Would you have said that? Don't you say it, every day? . . . We're all innkeepers, with room for everybody and everything but Him."

And that's how it was then. . . .

But if in your heart the Babe of Bethlehem has found lodging, now He has a place. Your loving response and your faithful witness secure for the Christ access to the hearts and minds of others who may also make room. But He uses people, and He chooses to use you, and in this experience of childbirth He is providing you with a new opportunity to show other "innkeepers" how they can "make room" for Him.

Don't crowd Him out!

*And there were in the same country shepherds abiding in the field, keeping watch over their flock by night.* LUKE 2:8

There is something terribly significant about the fact that the birth announcement was first made to lowly shepherds. He who was to become the great, good Shepherd was first seen by shepherds. But God is no respecter of persons: "Though the Lord be high, yet hath he respect unto the lowly . . ." (Psalm 138:6).

I'm glad the shepherds were told first. They came running, I'm almost certain, and they brought the gift of belief. Their hands were of necessity empty, poor shepherdfolk that they were, but their hearts were full of wonder. This was their gift to the Christ-child and to us—the precious intangible gift of wonder!

Pity those who do not wonder. The continuing radiance of wonder which first surrounded the shepherds, and has since reached into the hearts of all believers, has not penetrated the cold, questioning hearts of the doubters.

Let us simplify our lives to prepare our hearts for that which Christ has yet in store for us. For you, right now, this means the miraculous wonder of giving birth. Be like the shepherds; glorify and praise God. Will others wonder because of you?

Read Luke 2 in as many different versions as you can obtain.

107

*Glory to God in the highest, and on earth peace, good will toward men.* LUKE 2:14

There is a hospital in Hong Kong which came into being in a miraculous way. Dr. Bob Chapman and Dr. Gordon Addington, American medical missionaries, sensed the great need, exercised faith and good judgment, informed their mission board, prayed, and believed God would undertake; and today the inscription on the outside of that modern medical institution reads: "Glory to God—Peace Toward Men."

That was the refrain first uttered by the heavenly host announcing a Baby's birth, the message of which resounds through the corridors of time, still heralding the Good News. There has never been, nor will there ever be, another birth announcement like that one.

Have you planned your birth announcement? There are so many cleverly worded and attractive announcement cards available today. Or perhaps you will have something special printed. When our first two children were born, and because their proud father worked in a bank, our announcements were made in the form of a check drawn on the International Stork Bank. The third and fourth births found us in the Christian bookstore business, so our announcements were in the form of a book.

The inspiration for this book of meditations came with our little Volume No. 4. The "cover" for the book birth announcement read "Heritage of the Lord" and listed my husband and me as the "authors." The Publisher was God the Creator; copyright was "Before the Foundation of the World" (Ephesians 1:4); the first, second, and third editions were listed, with their birth dates, as well as the fourth edition. Special acknowledgment was made to the doctor for "editorial assistance" at the time of publishing, and contents were listed as follows:

I.     *Introducing Kraig Peter*
II.    *6 lbs. 9 oz. of "Baby Appeal"*
III.   *In Stature: 1 ft., 8 in.*

108

The preface read: "With joy we present this 'volume,' and a prayer that its 'pages' will bless and enrich others throughout its lifetime, to the glory of its Maker—*The Authors*. 'Lo, children are an heritage of the Lord . . . ,' Psalm 127:3a. 'For by him were all things created . . . ,' Colossians 1:16a." (The general outline of this birth announcement was included by request.)

*. . . they brought him to Jerusalem, to present him to the Lord.* LUKE 2:22

It was the custom, according to the Law of Moses, for Jewish parents of a newborn child to circumcise the child on the eighth day. This the parents of Jesus did. Then they brought Him to Jerusalem to present Him to the Lord. The old Levite Law required a sacrifice of a lamb and a pigeon, or two pigeons. The fact that Joseph and Mary offered the two pigeons indicates that they were very poor.

Old Simeon, whose heart was open to the Holy Spirit, and who was waiting with expectation for this very One, recognized in the Infant Jesus the Light of the World, the Promised One.

The day will come, the Lord willing, when you too will present your child to the Lord. For some this means infant baptism, for others dedication. Whichever it is for you, as parents let it be a time of rededication of yourselves to the One who is thy salvation.

Read Luke 2:21-39.

*And the child grew and became (spiritually) strong, filled with wisdom, and the grace of God rested upon Him.*

LUKE 2:40, BERKELEY

The Bible is silent about Jesus' early years, except for the incident in the Temple when He was twelve years old. We rather wish we had been given more of an insight into His home life, and we cannot accept as authentic the Apocryphal accounts of the childhood miracles Jesus performed. We are sure, however, from this Scripture that Jesus was the finest of young lads, conducting Himself as the eldest in a family of seven children.

What kind of a mother was Mary? We are certain that she was God-fearing, and that from His earliest childhood Jesus heard the Old Testament stories and learned the Biblical precepts at her knee. "Devout" and "sensible" are words which have been used to describe this dear mother.

Mary knew, as you and I must recognize also, that our children are really not ours. They belong to God. Such a sacred trust!

You will probably be reading many things concerning child development. Of course, you are anxious to do the right things for your child, and you will be looking to many outside sources for guidance and help. There are many excellent Christian books on this subject, written by doctors, psychiatrists, and others who have specialized in the subject of children and their development, and you will want to seek Christian guidance wherever possible. But God's own Word will be your invaluable aid. Without it, you will be left groping, incapable of leading your child so that he will experience God's grace, even as Jesus' did.

*. . . His mother treasured all these things in her heart.*

LUKE 2:51, PHILLIPS

Mothers have a way of treasuring in their hearts the things their children do and say. In later years the children take particular delight in hearing a mother repeat the stories over and over as she recalls the phrases they used and things they did. Mary, too, treasured much in her heart, but the memory of Jesus' first Temple visit in Jerusalem must have been of special significance.

"But why were you looking for Me? Did you not know that I must be in My Father's house?" (v. 49, PHILLIPS). Yes, that was what the twelve-year-old Jesus had said to His mother. Was Jesus giving her His first hint that He knew why He had been born? Mary must have had a sleepless night. She loved Jesus as her firstborn, and no doubt the tears trickled from her eyes during many sleepless nights as she pondered in her heart Jesus' future.

And that's the way it is for mothers. Their hearts hold the treasure of a child's precious sayings and actions; their hearts overflow with love and longing for the best for their children. A mother's heart cries out in the darkness of night to a heavenly Father for help and direction.

Read about the Temple incident in Luke 2:41-52. Ask God to magnify the capacity of your heart to receive in the days and years ahead the expressed thoughts of your child.

*And as Jesus continued to grow in body and mind, he grew also in the love of God and of those who knew him.*

LUKE 2:52, PHILLIPS

Every mother is anxious to record the growth of her little one. We take pride in their weight gain during those first few months. We have anxious moments when we feel they are not gaining as rapidly as we suppose they should. Regular visits to our doctor are loaded with questions, and his words of professional wisdom give assurance that we are not failing in our role.

But we shall fail, and miserably, if in succeeding years there is not a spiritual growth. Will our child love God? Our faithfulness in reading Bible stories, going with him to Sunday school and church worship services, and training him in the way he should go will do much to determine his growth as a child of God.

Will those who come to know him love him? His personality development, so closely linked to his spiritual understanding, is also yours to mold. Let the words of this Scripture

111

be a verse you claim for your child as with God's help you mother him.

*. . . and, as his custom was, he went into the synagogue on the sabbath day . . .* LUKE 4:16

Jesus has set the perfect example of conduct on the first day of the week. He went to the synagogue, as was His custom. This was the way He had been trained from His earliest years, and he was an obedient Son. He was obedient to His early training and, more important, obedient to what He knew the Scriptures declared.

A day of rest had been instituted at the time of creation. (Read Genesis 2:3.) After His resurrection Jesus met with His disciples on the first day of the week, and this is the day we observed as Sunday. This is the day we will want to train our children to set aside for worship and meditation. As a family we will go to Sunday school and church. We will go because we love Christ, and our minds need the spiritual rejuvenation that comes from remembering the Lord's day and keeping it holy.

There is something else here that stands out boldly. ". . . as his custom was . . ." is a little four-word phrase freighted with meaning. We are told that up to eighty percent of what a child learns is acquired in his preschool years. No parent can lightly dismiss those formative years.

How fortunate we are to be living in an age where the church nursery has been recognized as a vital part of the total church program. You will want to set this pattern early in your child's life.

Today read Hebrews 10. Meditate on verses 22—25.

*And he delivered him to his mother.* LUKE 7:15

The miracles Jesus performed showed His great compassion. Here we see Him showing sympathy for the widow of Nain,

112

whose only son had died. Elsewhere we see Him restoring life to Jairus' daughter. His acts of mercy towards those who were blind, lame, or afflicted revealed His love and concern for the sin-sick world into which He had come.

It is this same love, expressed by His physical presence while here upon earth, but available today through the power of His Holy Spirit, which He extends to us today. Let this speak assurance to your own heart today as your waiting days become fewer. In due time, God will deliver the child to you, its mother.

*But as many as received him, to them gave he power to become the sons of God, even to them that believe on his name: Which were born, not of blood, nor of the will of the flesh, nor of the will of man, but of God.* JOHN 1:12-13

*Of his own will begat he us with the word of truth, that we should be a kind of firstfruits of his creatures.* JAMES 1:18

*Being born again, not of corruptible seed, but of incorruptible, by the word of God, which liveth and abideth for ever.*
I PETER 1:23

*Behold, what manner of love the Father hath bestowed upon us, that we should be called the sons of God . . .* I JOHN 3:1

Begotten of God! Our hearts echo the praises spoken by the beloved Apostle John, the fisherman Peter, and Jesus' own earthly brother James. The birth of a child of God! How perfectly the Holy Spirit witnesses to our spirits that this has been our experience through the power of the Word.

Read Romans 8.

*Except a man be born again, he cannot see the kingdom of God.* JOHN 3:3

As Christian mothers we know that when the act of birth has been completed, this child must someday experience rebirth if he is to become a child of God. Physical birth is but the beginning. Jesus chose to reveal this to Nicodemus, a leader among the Jews, who came to Him at night.

We give our children back to the Lord in our hearts even before they are born. We trust God to have His perfect will in their lives, and we teach them the right way. From early childhood we read the Bible to them; we pray together. Our hearts thrill as they lisp their simple, trusting, little prayers; when they sing "Jesus Loves Me," and when they speak of Him. We note their growth in these ways with as much joy as their physical progress gives us. But always, in the deepest recesses of our hearts, there is the longing for the moment when they will experience being born again.

When one of our children, at the age of nine, made her commitment to Jesus, a little friend remarked, "But I thought you always were a Christian . . . ," to which Rhonda replied, "Yes, I loved Jesus, but now I've said it out loud and I really know!" And she really did know. It was her rebirth. What a joyous experience awaits the parents and the child. The "waiting" years are like the "waiting" months. We are especially careful about what we eat before the child is born. We know our diet and eating habits will affect the unborn child. After birth and through the years, as we await their rebirth, we nurture them in God's Word with great care. We feed their little minds and hearts upon the Bible truths. We prepare them for holy occupancy. When the moment of their rebirth arrives and the "waiting" years are over, we rejoice with an even greater joy than we experienced at the moment of their physical birth.

With our two daughters the "waiting" years were equal to the "waiting" months in number: both were nine years old. Some children will experience rebirth earlier, some later, some much, much later. How good it is to have a loving heavenly Father upon whom we can "wait"! With the Apostle John we can say, "I have no greater joy than this, to hear that my [spiritual] children are living in the Truth . . ." (III John 4, AMPLIFIED).

Read the entire third chapter of John's Gospel.

*. . . even before I was born God had chosen me to be His and called me—what kindness and grace—To put His Son within me so that I could go to the Gentiles and show them the Good News about Jesus . . .*

GALATIANS 1:15–16, LIVING LETTERS

Here the Apostle Paul is writing to the Christians in the churches in Galatia. His message is a passionate vindication of himself as having received the word of truth directly from the Lord Jesus Christ Himself. It is a stirring, forceful letter that strikes a warm responsive note in our hearts.

Just think—even before this child of yours is born, God has planned every detail of his life. We do not pretend to understand this completely. It is too much for our finite minds to comprehend. We accept it; we praise Him for it; and we love Him all the more. With Paul we would say to those who question, "Oh my children, how you are hurting me. I am once again suffering for you the pains of a mother waiting for her child to be born—longing for the time when you will finally be filled with Christ" (Galatians 4:19, LIVING LETTERS).

Read the Book of Galatians.

*Follow God's example in everything you do just as a much loved child imitates his father.* EPHESIANS 4:19, LIVING LETTERS

Paul is speaking to his spiritual children. Elsewhere he says, ". . . be followers together of me" (Philippians 3:17).

Mrs. Charles Mellis, devoted wife of the secretary-treasurer of Missionary Aviation Fellowship, a mother of three sons and one daughter, was asked to address a mother-daughter banquet when her daughter was still an infant. As she thought about what she should say, she projected her thinking to the day

115

her only daughter would be grown up. She remembered what Paul had said, and in her lovely "Letter to Esther" wrote:

"Maybe you thought I was doing all the teaching as you were growing up. But let me tell you some of the things you taught me. You taught me to guard my tongue—and even my thoughts and attitudes. I remembered what Paul had said to his spiritual children in Phil. 3:17: 'Be ye imitators of me', and I wondered . . . What would happen if I asked you to imitate me in the things I was consciously (or subconsciously) making important in my life? You see, you gave me a new perspective on my relationship to the Lord, in the value I was placing on: material 'things'; on the stewardship of not only money but *time*; on clothes; on friendships; on church loyalty—and even on work habits. You made me wonder too just how you would—someday—imitate me as a wife. I read and re-read the last half of Proverbs 31 which gives a pattern for a wife. Would you want the world's status for a woman (independence, equality)? Or would you want to do your shining through your husband? Would you want him known and appreciated because you had given of yourself? Here was a challenge to me: Was I making my role as a wife a living symbol of what Christ wants His bride (the Church) to be? If I would be imitated—I should be worth imitating. So you unknowingly pushed me into deeper Bible study and prayer. And Deut. 6:5-7 became an important goal.

" '. . . you shall love the Lord your God with all your heart, with all your soul, and with all your strength. These words with which I am now charging you shall be written on your heart; and you shall impress them deeply upon your children; you shall talk of them when you are sitting at home, while you walk on the road, when you lie down, and when you get up . . .' (BERKELEY).

"To me, this meant not only 'praying together' but 'playing together'—time set aside for baking and sewing—together— and for various forms of family recreation. To keep up with

116

you as your schooling progressed, I felt the need of wider reading—to speak intelligently with you and your friends—and to be ready with suggestions at times of counseling.

So you see, the Lord has used you to enrich my life—just as He has given me the privilege, as well as the responsibility, of being used in your life. And now that the apron strings are loosed, I can say with Paul in Phil. 1:6 (RSV) "I am sure that God Who began the good work within you will keep right on helping you grow in His grace until His task within you is finally finished on that day when Jesus Christ returns."

Read the Book of Ephesians.

*Let the enriching message of Christ have ample room in your lives as you instruct and admonish one another . . .*
COLOSSIANS 3:16, BERKELEY

The demands made upon mothers are great. It is easy to become "involved." The involvements can be taxing, so much so that the enriching message of Christ does not find ample room in our busy lives. When this happens, often without our awareness of what is taking place, family life suffers. Paul's admonishment that, as wives, we are to be submissive to our husbands finds us unwilling, even rebellious. It is difficult for our children to heed Paul's advice, "Children, be obedient to your parents in every respect, for so it greatly pleases the Lord" (v. 20, BERKELEY), for often our demands are unreasonable when we ourselves are "too busy" and "out of tune" with the Word. We make it hard for our husbands to love us, and resent it if they show harshness.

Yes, all of this is possible even for the Christian wife and mother who allows outside interests and involvements to deprive her of the enriching message of Christ which she can receive from daily communion with Him through prayer and the Word.

How can mothers best determine what to do and what not

to do for "outside interests"? God's Word has the answer. It is the verse found in this same chapter which can become your creed.

Read Colossians 3:23.

*So God sent pain and sorrow to women when their children are born, but He will save their souls if they trust in Him, living quiet, good and loving lives.*

I TIMOTHY 2:15, LIVING LETTERS

The place of women in the church is clearly defined by the Apostle Paul. He has been accused of being a woman hater; this, however, would appear to be unjust. For a clear understanding of such passages as those found in this chapter, it is important to realize the background against which it was written.

G. Campbell Morgan states: "Turning to the matter of the demeanor and position of women, we must remember that Paul was dealing with affairs in Ephesus. Behind the picture of the Christian woman as here portrayed is that of many of the women of the Greek communities, and it was to save the women of the Church from any conformity to debased ideals that these passages were written."

Paul's words of caution, however, seem entirely applicable to the society in which we live. The Phillips translation reads: ". . . women should be dressed quietly, and their demeanour should be modest and serious. The adornment of a Christian woman is not a matter of an elaborate coiffure, expensive clothes or valuable jewelry, but the living of a good life. A woman should learn quietly and humbly" (I Timothy 2:9-11).

Pain is a natural part of childbirth. The Bible explains it thus: "Nevertheless (the sentence put upon women [of pain in motherhood] does not hinder their [souls'] salvation), and they will be saved [eternally] if they continue in faith and love and holiness, with self-control; [saved indeed] through

118

the Child-bearing, that is, by the birth of the [divine] Child"
(v. 15, AMPLIFIED).

The pain of giving birth is quickly replaced with the joy
of receiving a child from the Lord—our very own baby!

I think that at one time or another a woman feels a sense
of guilt that it was one of her sex who brought about original
sin. And Paul reminds us of this very fact (v. 14). But even
though sin came into this world because of a woman, so did
our Saviour—and the Apostle recognizes this as well.

Read the Book of I Timothy and concentrate on Chapter 2.

*I know how much you trust the Lord, just as your mother
Eunice and your grandmother Lois do; and I feel sure you
are still trusting Him as much as ever.*

II TIMOTHY 1:5, LIVING LETTERS

Christians were being tested in the most severe ways. There
were arrests, imprisonments, persecutions, crucifixions, agonies
endured that make us shudder even as we read of them. And it
was then that Paul was again arrested and thrown into prison.
This letter, written in the darkest hour in the days of early
Christianity, cries out, but with assurance and triumphant
faith.

Paul is writing to his true son in the faith. He calls to
remembrance young Timothy's sincere and unqualified faith.
And where did he get this remarkable faith? Timothy, from
infancy, had been trained by his mother and grandmother.
First they instilled in him a love for God, as they were devout
Jews. When they learned that Jesus was the promised Messiah—no doubt through Paul's preaching—Timothy too came
to know and love Him.

What a wonderful young man Timothy must have been!
How pleased and proud—but more, how thankful—the mother
and grandmother must have been! When Paul said he needed
young Timothy, the mother-heart and grandmother-heart
must have pulsed with deep-felt and mixed emotions. They

loved him so! But they loved Paul, too. And they trusted Paul. They trusted God above all, and loved Him with unselfishness.

There is a beautiful message here for prospective mothers. Timothy grew up in a home filled with love, and this is what you will want to create in your home.

Ask God, right now, to show you how you can love your family in the right way. Continue in the days and years ahead to seek His guidance as you show forth your love. Ask Him to help you *not* to spoil or pamper your child, but to love him as He would have you do it. Then when the day comes, as it surely will, when this child must leave the shelter of love at home, both of you can face the unknown future with the same confidence Paul expressed as abiding in Timothy, Lois, and Eunice.

*And so we keep on praying for you that our God will make you the kind of children He wants to have—will make you as good as you wish you could be!—rewarding your faith with His power. Then everyone will give glory to the Name of the Lord. Jesus Christ because of the results they see in you, and your great glory will be that you belong to Him. For that is the way God and the Lord Jesus Christ have planned it.* II THESSALONIANS 1:11-12, LIVING LETTERS

You have now either reached the end of your "waiting" days, are approaching the end, or may already be holding in your arms your precious heritage of the Lord. Whatever your present "condition," we sincerely trust that this book of meditations has helped to make the experience an even happier one. Together we have seen God at work in the affairs of men as He first brought life upon the earth, as He multiplied and blessed the human race through the Old Testament patriarchs and their wives, supremely through the birth of the Lord Jesus, again through some of the New Testament families, and now right up to you.

Before you lies the most rewarding, and, at the same time,

the most demanding and time-consuming job in all the world —*motherhood!* But it is also the most joyous and the most glorious. Volumes have been written on the subject. With God's Word as our basic and prime guide, and Jesus' love as He showed it to little children as our pattern, we can echo Paul's words as our own lifelong prayer.

*A woman when she is in travail hath sorrow, because her hour is come: but as soon as she is delivered of the child, she remembereth no more the anguish, for joy that a man is born into the world.* JOHN 16:21

Joy! Wondrous joy! Unbelievable joy! Joy unspeakable! That is the feeling that floods our being, even as Jesus said, when we have finally given birth to the child.

Jesus was talking to the bewildered disciples. He was going to leave them to go to be with the Father, and this they could not understand. Their hearts were pained and they were sorrowful. "And ye now therefore have sorrow: but I will see you again, and your heart shall rejoice, and your joy no man taketh from you" (v. 22).

Yes, they did understand. It took time, anxious waiting, but they experienced the filling of the Holy Spirit and His enabling power.

Christ chose to explain to the disciples this great truth through an illustration which you can easily appreciate right now. He is aware of what it means for a woman to be with child. He is an all-knowing Saviour. The earthly cares and joys draw us still closer to Him. Someday our hearts will rejoice forevermore as we see Him, whom to know is life everlasting.